LEGACY

A Portrait of the Young Men and Women of
Kamehameha Schools
1887–1987

Bernice Pauahi Bishop

Legacy

A Portrait
of the Young Men and Women of
Kamehameha Schools
1887–1987

Written by
Sharlene Chun-Lum and Lesley Agard

KAMEHAMEHA SCHOOLS PRESS
HONOLULU, HAWAIʻI

PUBLISHED BY KAMEHAMEHA SCHOOLS PRESS
KAMEHAMEHA SCHOOLS
HONOLULU, HAWAI'I 96817

Edited by Glen Grant

Designed by Oliver Kinney

Produced by Marsha Heu Bolson

Project Photographers: Luryier "Pop" Diamond and Bruce Lum

Publication Consultant: David Rick

Library of Congress Cataloging in Publication Data

Chun-Lum, Sharlene, 1950–
Kamehameha Schools.

1. Kamehameha Schools—History. I. Agard,
Lesley, 1950–   . II. Title.
LD 7501.H825C48 1987   373.969'31   87-22527

ISBN   0-87336-009-5

Printed in Japan

First Printing 1987

CONTENTS

ACKNOWLEDGEMENTS

This Centennial portrait of the Kamehameha Schools is the result of time, information, and memories contributed by individuals too numerous to acknowledge separately.

However, we would like to thank the scores of Kamehameha graduates and staff (former and current) who so generously shared their recollections of life at the Schools over the last 100 years. As sources of information, Dr. Donald Kilolani Mitchell, the Kamehameha archives, annual reports, histories by Loring Hudson and Richard Greer, and detailed reports by Robert Springer were indispensable.

In addition, we were grateful for the comments and suggestions of the book's editorial hui: Neil Hannahs, Sherlyn Franklin, Tony Ramos, George Kanahele, Kihei de Silva and Marsha Bolson.

The staff of the Public Affairs Department: Harriet Oana, Amy Kahawai, Dawn Farm-Ramsey, Puanani Fernandez-Akamine, Kekoa Paulsen, and Sandy Putt, also provided invaluable assistance and support. A special mahalo goes to Marsha Bolson, Communications/Community Relations Manager, who coordinated the efforts of all those involved in the project, organized all book production details, extensively edited the manuscript and diligently proofread everything at least a dozen times.

Oliver Kinney is to be commended as much for his unruffled calm as for his artistry. Glen Grant deserves congratulations for succeeding in cutting copy to a quarter of its original length, and David Rick's reminders to look at the book objectively, the way a non-Kamehameha reader would, were appreciated.

Last, but certainly not least, thank you to all the photographers, past and present, who chronicled Kamehameha's story in pictures. Particularly important were the contributions by Luryier "Pop" Diamond who originated the idea for the book and kept meticulous photo files to make it possible, and Bruce Lum who added color to its pages.

The Authors

FOREWORD

A few years ago, as part of the effort to celebrate its 100th anniversary in 1987, the Kamehameha Schools Centennial Celebration Committee recommended that several authors be commissioned to write books about various aspects of Kamehameha.

As a graduate, I felt privileged to be asked to author a pictorial account of Kamehameha's first hundred years. However, it soon became apparent that this was an awesome task for one person working part-time so Lesley Agard, another member of the Class of 1968, agreed to work on the final two chapters. Even with two of us on task, we discovered that trying to cover 100 years in barely over 150 pages was overwhelming.

There is a wealth of photographic material being maintained in Kamehameha's Archives by Luryier "Pop" Diamond, who also served as the project's photo editor. The Hawaiian Collection and Midkiff Room in the Midkiff Learning Center also house thousands of articles and mementos. In addition, many graduates and staff members have interesting stories to tell. And as graduates ourselves, it was a challenge to keep our own experiences from coloring our account of special events.

The problem was not what to put in, but what could be left out. In the limited space we tried to focus on the unique experience that so many Kamehameha alumni remember fondly.

Through photographs, personal recollections and mention of significant events, we hoped to give all people interested in Hawaiian youth a sense of the contribution that Kamehameha has made in the lives of its more than 13,000 alumni and their families. We also wanted to show the evolutionary process which has made Kamehameha Schools the educational force it is today.

We hope this book will serve as a tribute to the Schools' founder, Bernice Pauahi Bishop, whose foresight created the Kamehameha Schools. Her estate continues to provide a brighter future for thousands of Hawaiian children through a number of educational programs.

This is just one of many books that could be written about the Kamehameha School experience. We hope that it will pique the readers' interest and evoke in them similar memories of their youth and educational experiences.

Sharlene Chun-Lum

Thirteenth. ... I give, devise and bequeath all of the rest, residue and remainder of my estate real and personal, wherever situated unto the trustees below named, their heirs and assigns forever, to hold upon the following trusts, namely: to erect and maintain in the Hawaiian Islands two schools, each for boarding and day scholars, one for boys and one for girls, to be known as, and called the Kamehameha Schools.

I direct my trustees to expend such amount as they may deem best, not to exceed however one half of the fund which may come into their hands,

Bernice P. Bishop

Honolulu; I also direct my said trustees to keep said school buildings insured in good companies, and in case of loss to expend the amounts recovered in replacing or repairing said buildings. I also direct that the teachers of said schools shall forever be persons of the Protestant religion, but I do not intend that the choice be restricted to persons of any

Chapter 1

Good and Industrious Men and Women

The Early Years

Kamehameha Schools began on an arid, barren tract of Pālama land on the outskirts of Honolulu. A few simple, wooden buildings including the Principal's Cottage, a kitchen, three two-story dormitories, outbuildings for washing and ironing clothes and a dining hall comprised the very first campus of the School for Boys.

On opening day, November 4, 1887, five teachers and nearly forty students prepared the campus for a royal fete. Bernice Pauahi Bishop's wish to establish a school for Hawaiian children had at last become reality. Hawai'i's leading citizens came to honor that legacy. King Kalākaua and Queen Kapi'olani arrived with a distinguished entourage. *Ali'i*, trustees, legislators and businessmen prayed that day for the School's success in imparting a superior education to generations of Hawaiian youth.

The students listened intently as His Majesty inspired them in their native language to uphold the name of Kamehameha. He extolled the value of workmanship and reminded them that their happiness in life was dependent on "the intelligence which sprang from doing any work well." The next day the *Pacific Commercial Advertiser* predicted that the Kamehameha School for Boys would "confer a lasting and ever-increasing benefit upon this community."

Though the campus in those early years was small, the vision was exciting and expansive.

Left: *In Article 13 of her will, written in 1883, Bernice Pauahi Bishop directed her trustees "to erect and maintain in the Hawaiian Islands, two schools...one for boys and one for girls, to be known as and called the Kamehameha Schools."*

Below: *Reverend William Oleson addressing the student body at the 20th anniversary of the Kamehameha School for Boys, or Manual School as it was then called.*

Above: Mrs. Bishop's estate was directed by five trustees. The first were (left to right): C. R. Bishop, S. M. Damon, W. O. Smith, C. M. Cooke and Reverend C. M. Hyde.

The first Trustees faced many financial challenges in fulfilling Princess Pauahi's vision. She had bequeathed to the Schools the vast Kamehameha lands which comprised one-ninth of the Hawaiian Kingdom, but the estimated value of the estate was only $414,000 with $18,000 in cash assets. By necessity, the first campus was clean and orderly, but unimpressive. The heat, dust, rocks, insects and weeds of the Pālama campus added to its reputation of being a "poor boys' school."

Yet, what the school lacked in appearance, it made up for in its commitment to provide a good education in English subjects, coupled with sound moral training. The first teaching staff consisted of the Principal, Reverend William Brewster Oleson, Mr. W. S. Terry who taught "carpentering and blacksmithing," and Mrs. Oleson, Miss Dressler and Miss C. Reamer who taught tailoring. Miss Andrews was hired as a matron to supervise the young boarders. The curriculum emphasized industrial training considered necessary for a Hawaiian to achieve personal and social success.

As Principal, business manager and teacher, Reverend Oleson heartily agreed with this outlook. He had been for many years the head of the Hilo Boarding School and was committed to giving every student "the makings of a livelihood and the makings of a life." To his students this extraordinarily energetic educator was admiringly known as *Ahi* or Fire. He could teach any class in school and often did so. He designed the school uniform, selected the school colors, and established the Kamehameha Schools Press. With the music teacher Theodore Richards, Reverend Oleson wrote the School for Boys' class song, "Sons of Hawai'i." He also had a passion for baseball. Under his coaching, the first school baseball team won a game against a visiting Chicago Nationals team.

Under Reverend Oleson's inspiration, life at the School for Boys was rarely dull.

Right: Teachers of the School for Boys gathered in 1898 with Principal Uldrick Thompson (seated far left) for a photograph. A diverse group, they came from all parts of the United States with college degrees from Wesleyan, Harvard, Brown, Pratt Institute, Worchester School of Technology and Oswego Normal.

> *Nearly every business man and every professional man of these islands was pleased when the Kamehameha Schools was organized. They believed young Hawaiians would be trained to do all kinds of mechanical and office work…They also believed a good percent would prove capable of filling positions of responsibility and showed interest by sending boys to Kamehameha and paying their expenses.*

Uldrick Thompson
Teacher and Principal
of the School for Boys, 1898–1901

Below: *The Boys School student body standing at attention during a review in front of Bishop Hall, circa 1891.*

Above: *Mr. Levi C. Lyman teaching the young men drafting and mechanical drawing in Bishop Hall, circa 1890.*

Right: *The first band, formed in 1893, played instruments that were either bought with money contributed by Trustee Cooke or borrowed from a local Portuguese band.*

Above: *Students working in the foundry, circa 1890. School machinery was built and repaired by the boys as part of their practical studies.*

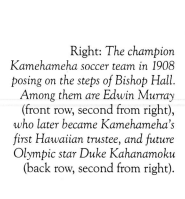

Above: *The first uniforms for Kamehameha boys were designed by Principal Oleson. The students were admired for their neat appearance, and often marched in local processions, parades and pageants.*

Right: *The champion Kamehameha soccer team in 1908 posing on the steps of Bishop Hall. Among them are Edwin Murray (front row, second from right), who later became Kamehameha's first Hawaiian trustee, and future Olympic star Duke Kahanamoku (back row, second from right).*

Students at the School for Boys had a demanding schedule of study and work with little leisure time. The day began at 5:30 a.m. as students cared for the buildings or grounds, prepared meals, set the breakfast table, cut wood, or cleared rocks and weeds. After breakfast and morning devotions, students spent half the day studying such subjects as arithmetic, algebra and geometry; English and penmanship; business and bookkeeping; mechanical drawing; geography and health. The remainder of the day was devoted to vocational shops where forging, woodturning, carpentry and pattern making were taught.

Students were always encouraged to give their new skills useful application. The print shop students published a newspaper, *The Handicraft*. In tailor shop, students made pillowcases, sheets, napkins, tablecloths, mosquito nets and mattresses for the School. The older boys sewed uniforms, khaki suits, jumpers and work shirts.

Not all school activities were work related. Music teacher Theodore Richards organized the first glee club in 1889 and thus started an enduring tradition. Sports were also popular, although the campus in those days was hardly suitable for athletic activity. The dry, dusty playing field was without a blade of green grass. "Rocks, rocks everywhere," remembers former teacher and principal Uldrick Thompson. Some of the boys finally put the rocks on the playing field to good use—they broke them up and sold them for ballast to outgoing ships!

Whether at study, work or recreation, the boys of Kamehameha were admonished to be "good and industrious men." Their lives were thus simple, routine and supervised. Discipline was demanded, but the rewards were to be for a lifetime.

Below: *A report card shows the diversity of subjects that were offered to the students in 1898.*

Above: *The grandfather clock built by Uldrick Thompson is carved with the names of class valedictorians on one side, and ROTC company commanders on the other. It now stands in Bishop Hall.*

Below: *In 1911, horseshoeing was added to the curriculum along with dairy farming.*

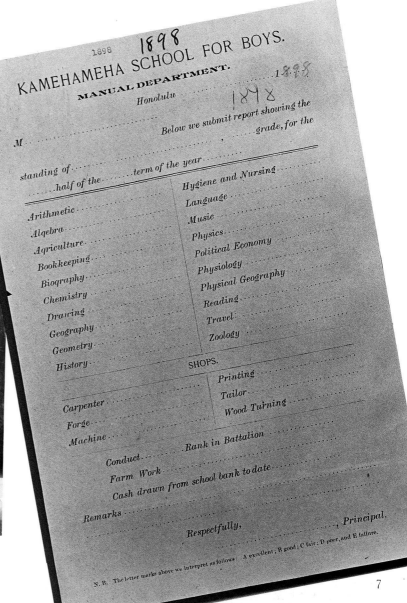

"Sons of Hawai'i"

Be strong and ally ye,
O sons of Hawai'i,
and nobly stand together
hand in hand.

All dangers defy ye,
O sons of Hawai'i,
and bravely serve your own,
your fatherland.

Ring, ring, Kalihi ring.
Swell the echo of our song.
Ray ray ray ray ray rah,
Ray ray, Kamehameha.
Let hills and valleys loud our
song prolong.

Kamehameha School Song
written by Principal
William B. Oleson
and music teacher
Theodore Richards

Right: *Members of the first graduating class of 1891 (seated left to right): John Waiamau, Samuel Keliinoi, William Crowell, Robert Pahau, Charles Blake, Thomas Haae; (standing left to right): William Keolanui, Fred Beckley, Solomon Hanohano, William Rathburn, Sam Kauhane, Moses Kauwe, Charles E. King, W. C. Enoch Brown.*

Young Hawaiian boys, ages six to twelve, were first given the chance to attend Kamehameha Schools in 1888 when a Preparatory Department was established. Charles Reed Bishop had provided the funds so that youngsters would be given "good morals, gentle manners, cleanliness of person and clothing and general surroundings."

One of the early principals of the Preparatory Department was Miss Nancy J. Malone, who in a short five years left her lasting mark on the department. As Uldrick Thompson recalls, "It is impossible to over-

Above: Use of both oral and written English was emphasized in Preparatory School classes such as this one in nature studies.

Right: The first Preparatory School was located at the present site of Farrington High School. The all-purpose main building, built in 1888, was a gift from Mr. Bishop.

estimate Miss Malone's devotion to her small charges. She was principal, teacher, matron, preacher, *luna* of the workmen in charge of grounds, and nurse."

Young preparatory students were given daily lessons in proper English, arithmetic, geography, nature studies, drawing, penmanship, health and singing. Good morals were promoted through the Sir Galahad Club which inspired chivalry in deed and thought. The boys were also encouraged to learn, whenever possible, through practical experience. In animal husbandry, for example, one class not only read about ducks but they raised, sold, killed, cleaned, cooked and ate them.

For those students who attended the Preparatory Department and the School for Boys, the Pālama campus became their home. It was here that they spent their youth, working, studying, playing and learning the necessary skills to enter adulthood with confidence. Ted Vierra, Class of 1919 and later a distinguished Island architect, entered the Manual School when he was only 10 years old. In his seven years at Kamehameha, he went home only four times. He asserts proudly that in those formative years the School offered him a "well-rounded education."

While steady progress was made educating Hawaiian boys, there remained the challenge of establishing a Kamehameha School for Girls as requested in Mrs. Bishop's will. Seven years after the opening of the School for Boys a similar campus was developed for girls. The outlook for its success was equally optimistic.

Above: Young boys designing patterns as a part of their elementary carpentry training.

Right: *The Preparatory boys tending their garden in which they raised fresh vegetables for the students' meals. Sometimes they sold the produce door to door in the community.*

Below: *Calisthenics and other athletic activities were a regular part of the school day.*

Above: *Evening prayers being said under the watchful eyes of the dormitory mother, circa 1897. Beds were lined up in rows to accommodate twenty or more boys. Each boy made his own mattress and stuffed it with as much straw as he desired.*

" *Whether we were mopping floors or working on projects in class, we learned to keep our feet on the ground and make ourselves useful.* "

Theodore Vierra,
Class of 1919

Above: Girls took four years of sewing to provide them with a useful skill for home or business. In later years, some girls earned their tuition or "pin" money by sewing dresses or making hats which they sold in the school store.

Princess Pauahi's birthday was honored in a special way when the Kamehameha School for Girls, located on King Street near the Preparatory school, celebrated its opening day on December 19, 1894. Thirty-five young female students and their principal, Miss Ida M. Pope, prepared to embark on the noble venture of female education.

At the turn of the century, proper education for a young woman meant training her for marriage and motherhood. Thus, girls thirteen years or older were taught how to run their own homes, or in some cases to become a wage earner. In addition to the academic classes in language, literature, geography, mathematics, psychology, history and elementary science, young ladies were taught the homemaking skills of sewing, cooking and laundering. Cleanliness and health care were emphasized with classes in nursing and hospital practice, and daily calisthenics.

In an effort to provide first-hand experience in proper childcare and housekeeping, a Senior Practice Cottage program was established in 1912. Students received training in running a household and taking care of children.

Above: *The Girls School campus was set among feathery algaroba trees. Vines, palms and giant bird nest ferns surrounded the buildings. The fountain located in front of the main building often served as the focal point for plays or music recitals by the students and faculty.*

Miss Ida Mae Pope,
Principal of the School for Girls,
1894–1914

Above: *Girls receiving instruction in science with modern microscopes and test tubes. Other subjects young ladies were offered included English, history, mathematics and vocational arts.*

Right: *The School for Girls' basketball team won the 1904 city championship. Sports were very popular with the young women of Kamehameha.*

16

For the boys and girls at Kamehameha, discipline, strength of character, moral pride, religious faith and practical skills were the cornerstones of their lives. The Hawaiian future would be dependent upon such young men and women who would successfully adapt to a changing Hawai'i.

Miss Pope was a principal, teacher, guardian, nurse and mother to her girls. Like Reverend Oleson, she was tireless in her devotion to the young women whose lives she was to shape. Formerly the head of Kawaiaha'o Seminary, she shared with Reverend Oleson the attitude that the responsibility of the teacher was to mold not only the intellect, but also the heart. Lydia Aholo, a member of the first graduating class, remembered Miss Pope, "whom we honored and loved," quite simply as a principal who "did everything."

Miss Pope's leadership inspired a high standard of moral conduct. The girls were closely supervised with a schedule of classes, chores and activities. They were given only one free day a month, which was frequently spent drawing, playing music, singing, reading or visiting the beach. Katherine Sadler Lowson, Class of 1905, recalls that during days off, "the young cadets in their uniforms would call on us or we would see them in chapel."

Below: *Domestic economy was required of all girls. According to Kate Sadler Lowson, Class of 1905, "We prepared our own meals regularly and learned to make specialty items such as jellies, jams and breads."*

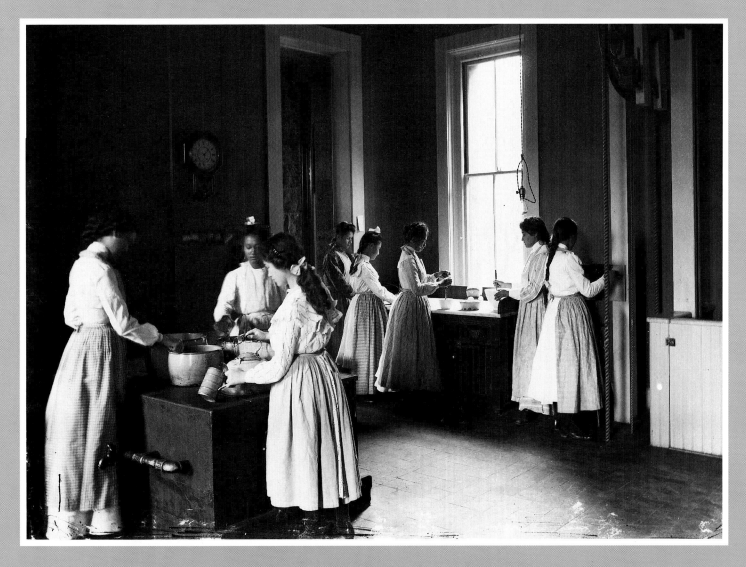

A Baobab tree stands today in front of Pākī Hall on the modern Kapālama Heights campus as a memorial to the early years. It was planted by the first graduates of the School for Boys, the Class of 1891, as a farewell gift to their beloved school.

The finest gift the young men and women graduates gave their alma mater in those years was becoming the "good and industrious men and women" envisioned by their benefactress. A survey by the School for Boys in 1914 revealed that of the two hundred and seventy-eight male graduates, nearly all were working as mechanics, clerks, teachers, agriculturists, architects, civil servants, musicians, deputy sheriffs or ranch managers.

Many were to become respected members of their community, such as Charles E. King, Class of 1891, who was a government worker, beloved musician and songwriter and Kamehameha Schools teacher. That same year, the School for Girls indicated that one hundred and sixty young women had been prepared to enter the community as productive homemakers with "noble traits of character."

The successes of these early Kamehameha graduates were achieved in the face of immense challenges. Hawai'i at the turn of the century offered fewer and fewer opportunities to its original inhabitants. If Hawaiian youth were to successfully bridge Old and Modern Hawai'i, then the vision of the Princess would need nurturing and growth.

Below: *Bishop Memorial Chapel was built by Mr. Bishop as a tribute to his wife. It was dedicated on December 19, 1897 and stood near where Farrington High School auditorium is today. Girls and boys regularly attended Sunday services there.*

"Pauahi Ke Ali'i"

Blest type of womanhood, So true, so pure, so good.
Thy praise we sing, thy praise we sing.

For bounteous gifts and free, in all around we see,
Of what God gave to thee, full hearts we bring.

Pauahi ke Ali'i, loyal we bend to thee,
Queen of our hearts, queen of our hearts.
Alohas loud resound, from all these hills around,
Where e'er thy name is found, where still thou art.

Cordelia Clymer Yarndley,
first music teacher at Kamehameha
School for Girls

Above: *The Class of 1897, the first
graduates of the School for Girls* (front
row, left to right): *Keluia Kiwaha, Jessie
Mahoakoa, Julia Lovell, Helen Kahaleahu,
Miriam Hale, Lewa Iokia, Lizzie Kahanu,
Julia Akana, Malia Kapali;* (back row,
left to right): *Kalei Ewaliko, Louise Aoe
Wongkong, Elizabeth Waiamau, Hattie
Kekalohe, Lydia Aholo, Lizzie Keliinoi.*

Pauahi O Kalani

Once each year on December 19, the anniversary of her birth, the Hawaiian youngsters of Kamehameha Schools gather to remember and honor Bernice Pauahi Bishop, the Hawaiian princess and founder of their school.

Just as they have since 1888, students dress in immaculate uniforms and white dresses, recite the words to Pauahi's favorite psalms and proverbs, and raise their voices in traditional songs of praise to their princess.

Noho ana ka wahine i ke anu o Mānā,
Mahalo i ka nani nohea o ka nahele.

E ola o Kalani, 'e Pauahi lani nui!
A kau i ka puaāneane.
E ola o Kalani, e Pauahi lani nui!
E ola loa no a, kau i ka wēkiu.

There she stays, our lady, in the cool clime of Mānā,
Admiring all its beauties, the glories of the forest.

Live, Oh Highness, Pauahi, royal great!
'Til time shall no more
Live, Oh Highness, Pauahi, royal great!
Live long, in truth, supreme in excellence!

"Pauahi O Kalani"
composed by Queen Lili'uokalani in honor
of her foster sister Pauahi

The annual gathering at Mauna 'Ala, the royal resting place of Hawaiian ali'i, is one of joy, not sadness. Each Founder's Day is a living tribute to a woman whose timeless vision and enduring legacy continues to benefit each new generation of Hawaiian children.

Above: *Each year, selected hymns and psalms are memorized and recited by students to honor Mrs. Bishop's memory.*

Right: *Students Milton Lai and Puanani Mundon, and President Harold Kent pay tribute to Mrs. Bishop at Founder's Day services held in the School's auditorium in 1954.*

Left: *"In the presence of the ashes of our Ali'i,"* begins the solemn pledge of respect recited by generation after generation of reverent students. Photo 1961.

Above: *The 120-year old decorative ironwork fencing surrounding Mauna 'Ala was ordered by Kamehameha IV from the prestigious Coalbrookdale Company in England.*

Left: *Norma Jean Lau Kong, Sherri Orton, Debbie Downey, and Ivalee Kamalu, all members of Kamehameha's Nā Wahine Hele Lā O Kaiona hula club, participated in the 1986 Founder's Day service at Mauna 'Ala.*

Above: *Wendell Huddy and Marie Valpoon place flowers on the Kamehameha royal family tomb in 1959.*

Above: *Today, services at Mauna 'Ala are made more comfortable by the addition of canvas canopies which protect participants from the unpredictable Nu'uanu showers.*

Right: *Preparatory Department students held their own Founder's Day services. Second graders Jina Hugo and Edward Simeona pose with a portrait of Bernice Pauahi Bishop in this 1963 photo.*

Right: Floral ho'okupu of all kinds are offered at the Princess' resting place each December 19.

Above: Waikahe, a musical ensemble comprised of Kamehameha graduates, performed at Founder's Day services in 1984.

Right: In the early years, the entire Kamehameha student body gathered at the Royal Mausoleum to pay their respects to the Schools' founder. Today, school-wide services are held at Kekūhaupi'o.

Chapter II

Kamehameha on the Move
The Twenties and Thirties

The banner headline of the *Honolulu Advertiser* on May 17, 1925 announced news both exciting and visionary: "Millions to be Spent on a New Plant for Kamehameha Schools." The Trustees had hired the famous architectural firms of C. W. Dickey of San Francisco and Bertram G. Goodhue of New York to draw plans for a campus "beautiful in architecture and preserving all Hawaiian traditions."

The cost of the new complex was to be between two and five million dollars. Several sites were being considered in Kahala and Mānoa Valley, but sentiment seemed to favor the hill above the Pālama campus, Kapālama Heights, where the "remoteness from the outside world" was considered "advantageous for study."

Modern buildings in a beautiful, spacious setting would enrich the students' education, and allow more Hawaiian children to enroll. Only three hundred students could be accommodated at the Pālama campus, and an increasing number were turned away every year.

The campus on Kapālama Heights was planned to house six hundred and fifty boarders and accommodate an equal number of day students. At least five hundred elementary school children could be enrolled. More importantly, there would be room for future expansion.

This commitment was a bold dream for a school that had, a decade before, been considered the "poor boys' school." But these were the Roaring Twenties and prosperity, expansion and bold thoughts were in the air. "Honolulu is growing,"

Trustee Albert Judd explained, "and the growth of Honolulu will always determine the growth of Kamehameha Schools."

This spirit of growth also imbued the Schools' new leadership. In 1923, the Trustees had appointed a young educator named Frank E. Midkiff to be the President of Kamehameha. A former master teacher at Punahou School and successful business executive with Lewers & Cooke, Ltd., Midkiff combined his business and teaching experience with a zeal for educational reform.

Convinced that Kamehameha Schools should be lifted to a level equal to private ivy league colleges such as Cogswell or Antioch, President Midkiff eagerly sought to expand and upgrade school programs. Under his leadership, a series of academic and vocational innovations were initiated that would make Kamehameha Schools one of the more progressive institutions in the Hawaiian Islands.

Left: *The School for Girls opened on the Kapālama Heights campus in 1931.*

" If we passed inspection and had no demerits, we could leave campus at noontime. We'd get all dressed up in our long-sleeved, grey uniforms and ride the trolley car downtown to go to the movies. "

William Kea
Class of 1927

Below: Cadet officers posing for a yearbook picture in 1927. The military played a prominent part in the life of Boys School students.

Above: In 1924, girls still attended classes on King Street in an all-purpose building that housed dormitory rooms, the dining hall and classrooms.

Left: Boys in the Preparatory Department posing in their white uniforms. The students always looked their best for chapel and special occasions.

Top: *In the 1930s, auto shop was a popular course among students. Some boys got apprenticeships at local businesses such as Schuman Carriage.*

Above: *Students in electricity class used modern equipment and methods to learn how to read meters even before most homes in Honolulu had electricity.*

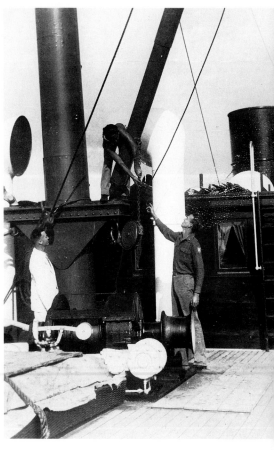

Right: *Some students in the 1930s signed up for nautical training.*

President Midkiff declared that compared to other colleges or universities in 1925, Kamehameha Schools had the finest record of placing graduates in vocations for which they had been trained. Midkiff was determined that Kamehameha maintain and improve its eighty percent placement record.

Innovations in the teaching of vocational skills were strongly encouraged. The best example of this was the "part-time system." Rather than going to school full-time, students were paired up and placed in a single "real world" job where they learned a trade by working with experienced craftsmen. One boy attended school for two weeks while the other worked. On the Saturday before they switched, they reviewed the work so that the job could be continued without interruption. At the Pearl Harbor naval yards, Hawaiian Electric, Mutual Telephone, the *Honolulu Advertiser*, Schuman Carriage and numerous plantations, the boys earned wages while acquiring a practical education.

Left: *Boys in Mr. Clarence V. Budd's electricity class learned to hook up electrical power lines.*

Vocational classes were constantly being refined to prepare students for new occupations and community needs. As Honolulu grew in size, so did the need for law enforcement. Consequently, students were trained for police work. By the mid-thirties, seventeen Kamehameha graduates worked for the Honolulu Police Department.

Interest in the printing profession also increased. Working on modern presses, students printed a variety of school materials including *The Cadet*, a student newspaper which became *Ka Mōʻī* in 1931. The printing experience gave some students a life-long trade. David Bray, Sr., Class of 1928, for example, became a printer foreman at the *Honolulu Star Bulletin*. Unique vocational training also became available as a few Kamehameha School students traveled to the Pacific Equatorial Islands to assist the United States military in the construction of airplane landing strips and refueling stations.

Below: *Students printing the school newspaper and annual in the Schools' printshop. The boys learned on presses that matched or surpassed what was used in commercial shops.*

With sugar production the largest industry in Hawai'i at this time, and Hawaiian homesteads becoming available, many educators and proponents of agricultural interests hoped that Hawaiian youth would rediscover the virtues of working the land.

At the Kamehameha School for Boys, this renewed emphasis on agriculture was illustrated by the 1925 opening of a farm school in Haha'ione Valley. Fifty acres of Bishop Estate land were set aside for training students in a variety of agricultural skills. Eventually the complex would comprise three hundred acres that included a dairy, piggery and hennery. With modern technical assistance from the Hawaiian Sugar Planters' Association and the University of Hawai'i, students raised cattle and grew alfalfa and other crops in the valley while taking courses in soils, plant life, animal life and husbandry, nursery practice, forestry and sugar production.

Despite faculty and industry encouragement, not many students were enthusiastic about pursuing a

career on the plantations. Skilled trades in the city were considered more desirable. With dwindling student enrollment and a lack of parent support, the Haha'ione Valley Farm was closed in 1934. Agricultural training continued at Kamehameha, but thereafter on a much smaller scale.

Top: *Haha'ione Farm was an agricultural training complex opened on Bishop Estate land in Haha'ione Valley. This view of the farm was taken in 1932.*

Above: *Herman Scholtz standing by the School truck used to take fresh produce and milk from the Haha'ione Farm to the Schools' main campus 16 miles away.*

Above: *Students raised livestock, among them this registered Aberdeen Angus bull.*

Above right: *Pineapple was one of the major crops raised on Haha'ione Farm. Working with the University of Hawai'i and Hawaiian Sugar Planters' Association, students experimented with a variety of pineapple farming methods and sold their produce to the canneries.*

Above left: *Charles Aina, Gus Sproat, William Coelho (kneeling left to right) and Sam Vida posing with their prize chickens, circa 1924.*

In fact, following the appointment of President Homer Barnes in 1934, the entire emphasis on vocational training underwent serious reassessment. Barnes, who had been Principal of the School for Boys, replaced Frank Midkiff who later became a Trustee. Believing that Kamehameha should remain a boarding school with a college preparatory climate, President Barnes resisted efforts to open the campus to day students. Instead, he stiffened academic requirements for admission and strengthened the academic curriculum. The pursuit of a college education and upward social mobility became strong goals for the young men of Kamehameha.

As Kamehameha boys were encouraged in the thirties to prepare for a college education, young ladies at the School for Girls continued their preparation to be good wives, mothers and wage earners. Household management, weaving, dietetics, cooking, sewing, millinery and nursing were but a few of the domestic arts offered.

In the Senior Practice Cottage, students were required to plan and cook meals, do household chores and even care for a baby. It was a forward-looking educational experience that generations of graduates would fondly remember.

The economic hardships of the Great Depression required wives to supplement the family income, so Kamehameha girls were taught how to earn money at home. Cooking class concentrated on how to turn a profit from homemade jams, jellies, candies and baked goods. In sewing

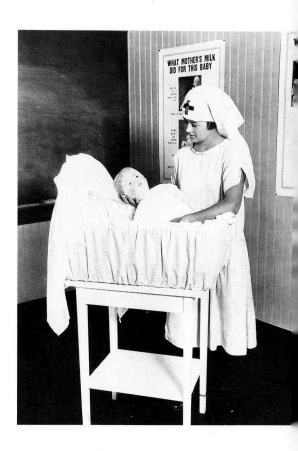

classes, senior girls made all their garments for graduation—from their bras and petticoats to their dresses. An income from dressmaking would greatly ease the household budget.

Girls were also offered the choice of preparing for teaching, clerical or nursing careers. Stenography and typing classes became popular as students gained experience working in the Schools' or Estate's offices. Students training to become teachers were placed as assistants in public and private kindergartens. As the role of women was slowly changing in Hawai'i, Kamehameha Schools endeavored to respond to these new trends and challenges.

Right: *Students in home economics used dolls to practice the basics of child-rearing. When the new Senior Cottage was completed, it featured the latest cooking and housekeeping equipment, and a live baby.*

Below: *Girls working towards a Commercial degree took typing and other business skills courses, circa 1920.*

Left: *Kamehameha girls were offered lessons in piano, orchestra and glee club. Public recitals were common. Dorothy Kahananui Gillett, Class of 1936 and Professor Emeritus in Music at the University of Hawai'i, recalls that "we were always preparing for some special program—Christmas, Founder's Day, Song Contest or Spring Concert."*

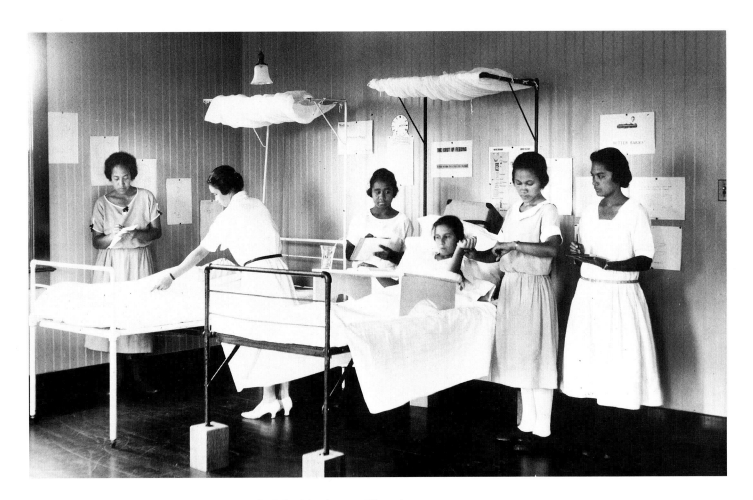

Above: *Girls got practical nursing training in the Schools' infirmary. They also went out to clinics throughout Honolulu such as Palama Settlement, where they assisted the regular nurses on staff. "In a way, we were interns in that we helped weigh the babies and got to listen to the advice nurses were giving the mothers about child care," recalls Dorothy Kahananui Gillett.*

Right: In 1918, the Kamehameha Warriors football team defeated all its opponents without allowing a single point to be scored against them!

Blue and White is Waving

Blue and white is waving;
Boys, we're back of you.

On our way to victory,
We'll be ever true.

Eager eyes are watching;
Hearts are beating fast.

For Kamehameha,
FIGHT, boys to the last!

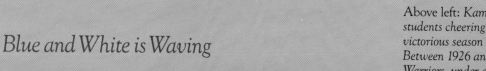

Above left: Kamehameha students cheering another victorious season on the gridiron. Between 1926 and 1937 the Warriors, under coach Bill Wise, won six city football championships.

Above right: Kamehameha cadets often were skilled in "non-traditional" arts. James Apo, Class of 1924, learned to knit sweaters in his free time.

Above: Girls enjoyed a progressive physical education program. Basketball, soccer, field hockey, gymnastics, tennis, and croquet were just a few of the sports offered. Photo circa 1920.

Left: Social activities were always strictly supervised. On Saturday nights, boys and girls could spend a few hours together singing songs or playing games under the watchful eyes of their housemothers. Photo circa 1929.

Above: *The Class of 1891 gathered for a 1930 reunion photograph in front of their class gift, the Baobab tree, now standing on the Kapalama campus.*

Kamehameha Schools in the twenties and thirties was on the move and nowhere was this more evident than in the spirit of campus life. While the Schools remained more conservative than co-educational campuses, social clubs had become extremely popular. Younger girls frequently joined the Girl Scouts while the young women became members of the *Hui Kumulipo.* Boys joined the Hawaiian club *Hui 'Ōiwi* which was organized by Donald Kilolani Mitchell and promoted Hawaiian culture, with special emphasis on games. Hawaiian language was taught by John Wise, and self-improvement groups such as the Posture club and Sub-Debs encouraged good grooming, personal neatness and proper attire.

Oratory, debate and literary societies were especially active. The Alumni Declamation Contest, renamed the Alumni Oratorical Contest in 1923, was attended by all students. The Quill and Scroll Society begun by teacher Loring Hudson was a popular literary group

of young journalists who wrote for the *Ka Mōʻī* or designed the yearbook. By the mid-thirties boys and girls were active in league sports as well as intramural sports, Hi-Y, Glee Clubs and National Honor Society. On the playing field, the Warriors made a name for themselves in their yearly battles against McKinley, Punahou and St. Louis high schools.

The most exciting special event enjoyed annually by Kamehameha students was the inter-class Song Contest first held at the School for Boys on November 20, 1920. That first contest was held outdoors with nothing but automobile headlights to light the "stage" on the Bishop Hall steps. The musical talents of Kamehameha students became so well known that they were asked to perform yearly on KGU radio at Christmas time and at Easter Sunrise Service in Punchbowl Cemetery. By 1940, radio station KGMB was airing the Song Contest island-wide under the sponsorship of Hawaiian Electric Company.

The Kamehameha spirit of pride

was symbolized in the School for Boys' Fiftieth Anniversary celebration on November 4, 1937. President Barnes presided over the festivities highlighted by a reunion of the first graduating Class of 1891 and a special address by Colonel Curtis P. Iaukea, Court Chamberlain to King Kalākaua. Colonel Iaukea recalled for the students that first opening ceremony half a century before which he attended with His Majesty.

The progress made by the Schools in the fifty years since that beginning was striking. Although the economic depression had curtailed full expansion and contributed to the closing of the Preparatory Department, student enrollment of nearly three hundred and fifty represented a tenfold increase. Over 1,200 men had graduated from Kamehameha.

Academically, the School for Girls ranked 2nd and the School for Boys 3rd in the Territory in oral English and theme writing for University of Hawai'i entrance exams. The School for Boys Kapālama Heights campus featured a new dining hall, two-story classroom building, auditorium, library, assembly hall, office, infirmary and seven dormitories. The number of applicants for admission to the school far outnumbered the spaces available.

By 1940, Kamehameha Schools was recognized as a first-rate, comprehensive secondary institution, providing a diverse, realistic vocational and academic program in a total learning environment. The future looked bright. The students and faculty of Kamehameha Schools could not imagine that within a year they would be embroiled in a war that would transform their generation, their Island home and their beloved school.

Below: *A Kamehameha cadet and sponsor surveying the Kalihi Valley view from the Kapālama Heights campus. Noted architect C. W. Dickey designed both the Haleakalā classroom building* (right) *and the W. O. Smith Library in a "Hawaiian style."*

Left: Kamehameha cadets parade through downtown Honolulu, circa 1920.

Left: The Kamehameha color guard precedes the battalion across Mawaena Field in a 1962 parade.

Right: A member of the JROTC cadet honor guard at his post during the 1982 Founder's Day service at the Royal Mausoleum.

Esprit de Corps

Ranks of stalwart, young Hawaiian cadets stand at attention on the sweltering parade ground. The cut of their hair, the pleat of their trousers, the shine of their brass shows diligent regard for detail. Their performance of the 208-count "Silent Manual of Arms," each movement an act of precision, demonstrates the rigid discipline and self-control they have learned.

Nearly one hundred years of military influence at Kamehameha has touched the lives of generations of young men, teaching them good conduct, self-discipline and leadership. From walking penalty tours with an M-1 rifle to proudly displaying field ribbons on a neatly pressed dress blue uniform, ROTC at Kamehameha provided memorable experiences for many Hawaiian youngsters.

Today, while those experiences play a less pervasive role in contemporary student activities, the lessons in self-reliance, responsibility and personal integrity are still valid. All freshman and sophomore boys attend military science classes, while upper classmen and girls enroll in ROTC by choice.

In accordance with Mrs. Bishop's wish that her schools produce "good and industrious men and women," the military tradition at Kamehameha continues, offering both boys and girls opportunities for scholarships, military institute appointments or a meaningful career.

Right: Cadets Piltz, Foo Sum, Meyer and Cordes test their map reading skills as a part of a 1956 military science class.

Right: Cadets set up for target practice at Schofield Barracks firing range in 1960.

Left: First aid and lifesaving techniques were taught in ROTC classes during the late 1950s.

Above: ROTC officers pose with sponsors on Bishop Museum steps, circa 1930.

Left: In the 1970s, girls were allowed to enroll in ROTC as an elective class. Photo 1973.

Above: *The drill team practices maneuvers on Mawaena Field in 1979.*

Below: *Class of 1970 freshmen get encouragement to maintain proper military demeanor from cadet Captain Charles Holderbaum in 1967.*

Chapter III

Warriors in the Modern World
The Forties and Fifties

The girls stood on their dormitory *lānai* and watched the billowing black smoke rise from Pearl Harbor shipyard as dive bombers swirled in the sky. Julia Stewart Williams, Class of 1946, recalls that they at first thought the bombing was "just another practice." But as the antiaircraft guns pumped the sky with bursting shells and fragments began falling on campus, it became quickly evident to them that "this was the real thing."

Shell fragments, machine gun bullets and misfired antiaircraft shells rained dangerously from the sky over Honolulu that Sunday morning. Four live shells actually fell on Kamehameha's campus, one striking at

Maluna Athletic Field. Students hastily packed their clothes to go home; staff anxiously listened for news on the radio. Maude Schaeffer, the Principal of the School for Girls, fetched two old, rusty guns with which she intended to protect her girls.

On the evening of December 7, 1941, students were crowded into the safest portions of the school halls, sleeping on improvised pallets. Each young woman carefully wrote her name, home address and parents' name on a white identification bandage that was then taped to her right shoulder. The next morning, most of the students were sent home. Thirty-six of the School for Boys

Cadets in formation in front of the Boys School Dining Hall before their departure for the Armed Forces Day parade, May 23, 1953.

43

Above: *In the days after the December 7, 1941 attack on Pearl Harbor, Bill Puniwai (left) and Curtis Kamai, both Class of 1944, were among the handful of cadets who stayed on campus to guard facilities such as the water tanks.*

students and faculty volunteered to remain on campus to guard the facilities.

A month later, the school reopened, but the war had greatly altered campus life. In the first months of World War II there was an acute need for hospitals, additional civilian defense headquarters and areas for evacuated civilians and dependents. Kamehameha Schools was thus occupied by the military as evacuees from Pearl Harbor, Wheeler, Schofield, and other military bases began arriving on the hill. Liholiho Dormitory was the first occupied. Eventually the army took over several Boys School buildings including Hale Ola, ʻIolani, Kapuāiwa, a section of Lunalilo Hall, and the entire Girls School campus.

The Provisional Hospital No. 1 was housed in Lunalilo Hall. Huge red crosses were painted on the hall's roof to let the enemy know it was a hospital. Mainly used for the wives and children of servicemen, the hospital was geared to service non-combatant medical needs. More than a dozen babies were delivered during those early months. Students in the School for Girls who had been given nurses training were asked to make beds and clean rooms. The young men served as orderlies.

Blackouts, air raid drills, bomb shelters and mock gas attacks became regular exercises. Many students who were over seventeen had enlisted in the army. Senior class students were asked to work full-time and juniors part-time in the homefront effort.

Since the Army occupied the upper campus, the girls shared the School for Boys facilities, creating an atmosphere of co-education. The young ladies helped in the war effort by organizing defense stamp drives, knitting garments for boys on the frontlines, hosting at the USO canteens or planting victory gardens.

As World War II drew to a victorious close, Kamehameha Schools looked optimistically to a future of peace and prosperity. Sacrifices had been made—loved ones and schoolmates lost on the battlefields of Europe or the Pacific Islands. Yet new economic and political opportunities offered themselves to Hawaiian youth who had the training, motivation and drive to succeed.

Below: *Two cadet guards catching a few winks between watches in a makeshift tent on campus in February, 1942.*

Right: *President Homer Barnes, Preparatory School Principal Lela Brewer (center) and several students accepting the Minute Man flag from Pauline Wollaston of the War Finance Department on October 22, 1943. The Boys School and the Girls School also won the award for their outstanding contributions to war bond and stamp campaigns.*

Below: *During World War II, the United States Army occupied several of the Pālama campus facilities for training recruits or housing civilian workers. The barbed wire protection around the buildings was a stark reminder of the impact of war on Island life.*

The post-war era was a time of expansion at Kamehameha Schools. Under the presidency of Colonel Harold Kent, the Schools in 1946 committed itself to effective vocational and college training and opened the campus to day students. As a consequence, the student enrollment of the School for Boys would eventually leap from 400 boarding students to 1,760 boarding and day students. At the School for Girls, enrollment was to grow from 218 to 418 students, half of whom were day students.

The Preparatory Department, which closed in the thirties, reopened in 1943 and began to enroll day students. Under Principal Lela Brewer, it offered instruction for three hundred and fifteen students on two campuses. Children in grades four through seven attended classes in Bishop Hall. Kindergarten through grade three classes were held at McNeil Hall with Blossom Nary

Above: *Seventh grader Terrance Zane displaying his science project, circa 1949. Students received a strong background in solid academic subjects such as science, math and English.*

Below: *Girls playing volleyball in their physical education uniform—palaka print shorts and tops. Girls wore neat and simple dresses to class while boys were attired in white shirts and khaki pants. Shoes and ties were optional wear for students below the seventh grade.*

Below: *A typical kindergarten classroom featured open spaces for the students to participate in group activities. From 1943 to 1955 students in grades K to 3 attended classes in a reconditioned Japanese language school on McNeil Street in Kalihi. Photo circa 1952.*

in charge. Principal Brewer, with a staff of twenty-eight teachers, put a priority on hiring qualified part-Hawaiian teachers or those with local teaching experience. Among those hired were Dorothy Kahananui Gillett, Class of 1936, and Mary Kawena Pūku'i.

Instruction for the young children was both progressive and innovative. Diagnostic tests were regularly given to students so that teachers were kept aware of their strengths and weaknesses. In an attempt to eliminate what were then considered to be the social disadvantages of "pidgin," proper use of English was stressed. The children were, however, given a keen awareness of their ethnicity through the development of Hawaiian studies materials. It became a regular practice to celebrate with pride the birthdays of *ali'i*, and speakers on a variety of topics would address the children at weekly assemblies.

As the successes and reputation of the Preparatory Department grew, so too did the desire of Hawaiian parents to enroll their children. New Preparatory Department buildings were finished in 1955 on the Kapālama Heights campus and 511 students in grades K-8 were enrolled. Five years later the number had grown to 800. The education of the younger Hawaiian children had at last been reestablished with an outstanding, pace-setting curriculum.

Above: *Fourth graders making traditional offerings to the god Lono during their Makahiki festival, circa 1952.*

Right: *Storyteller Caroline Curtis entranced and inspired a generation of Kamehameha students with Hawaiian legends. Photo circa 1959.*

Above: *First grade carpenters learning through doing at the McNeil Street campus.*

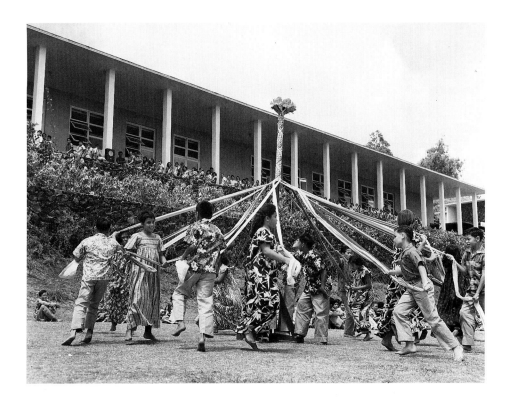

Left: *Students celebrating May Day on the new Preparatory campus, which opened in 1955. It featured thirty classrooms, a library, dining hall, administrative offices, infirmary and a beautiful view of Honolulu. Photo circa 1957.*

Study hall in
W. O. Smith library.

Above: *Ula Sheecha's Current Affairs class offered students challenging academic work. Photo circa 1952.*

Below: *Members of the Library Club helping to process books in the Schools' bindery.*

The School for Girls in the fifties also pursued a progressive curriculum. In addition to the traditional domestic training, girls at Kamehameha were encouraged to develop business and technical skills. Home economic courses no longer only taught sewing and cooking. Students now learned how to plan a wedding, create and maintain a budget, and select an insurance plan. They also learned the steps involved in buying a home, from valuing land to applying for a loan. Proper medical care, hygiene and etiquette were also stressed in an effort to shape socially adept women.

Practical experience was still obtained in the Senior Cottage Home program. As Kuulei Sequeira Stender, Class of 1950, recalls, the Senior Cottage helped her to become a good mother. While some of her peers knew nothing about raising a baby, she was skilled at taking temperatures, bathing and feeding an infant. "I hadn't cared for a baby before, but the Senior Cottage experience made me feel more comfortable about it."

The School for Girls' curriculum was divided at this time into three tracks: General, Commercial or College Preparatory. Using a variety of measures, including standardized test scores, the students were placed in the appropriate track. The results were encouraging. Many girls who were in the College Preparatory or "Imua" track found that they could perform competently at mainland universities. Girls in General or Commercial tracks readily found jobs. Kamehameha Schools had given them the foundation upon which to build a successful life.

Above: At the girls school store, boarders learned to do their own shopping and banking. Students could withdraw up to $2 a week from their accounts. Photo circa 1950.

Above: The Girls' Glee Club performing in 1950. The group performed in some forty public events annually.

Above: *Juniors and seniors working on Ka Mōʻī, the school newspaper, during a 1948 newswriting class.*

Left: *Field hockey was one of the intramural sports girls participated in after school. "We played team sports such as basketball, volleyball or softball twice a week," recalls alumnus Orpha Kinney Beirne, class of 1955.*

Above: *Seniors Daryl Jean Choo and Dayle Pescaia passing the time in front of Konia, the main classroom building at the School for Girls. The building was completed four years before this 1955 photo was taken.*

Right: *On a clear day, students in art class in Konia had the panorama of Honolulu as their subject. On cold and rainy days, fog enveloped the campus in a magical mist. Photo circa 1956.*

Above: *Senior Cottage students (left to right) Anna Sam, Annie Wong, Betty Mae Freitas and Amy Kalili show off the cottage babies in 1954.*

The Girls' School athletic pin was designed by Julia Stewart Williams in 1946 when she was a senior. Julia and other girls were awarded the pin for outstanding achievement in athletics.

Left: *Ninth grade students were introduced to archery in physical education class. "I gained a lifelong appreciation for all kinds of sports," states Daryl Jean Choo Pescaia, Class of 1955.*

Students practicing for the All School parade on Mawaena Field, May, 1953. Day and night parades were well attended by families, friends and invited guests.

The School for Boys in the postwar decades reestablished a polished image with new, neatly pressed military uniforms. President Kent firmly believed that the foundations of a successful life were built upon regulated behaviors. By 1952 the Junior Reserve Officer Training Corps (JROTC) had been renewed and Kamehameha was an approved Military Institute. War maneuvers and Officer Candidate School were part of the program as was a demerit system which was used in all phases of school life.

Under the influence of JROTC, school started promptly at 7:45 a.m. with a series of solid subjects, vocational arts, electives, devotions, military drills and assemblies following through the day to 4:15 p.m.

Communication skills were constantly stressed with remedial and honor speech classes offered. Each student was given a copy of *The Blue Book*, which was a manual of rules and behavior. The 1956 edition contained 90 pages of information, including the duties and proper dress and behavior of all cadets. Infractions of the rules resulted in demerits.

JROTC flourished at Kamehameha Schools during the fifties as the boys consistently ranked first in the JROTC Field Day held at the Honolulu Stadium. Because the school was designated an Honor Military Institute, three honor graduates could be nominated to attend the U.S. Military academies. Although the tone of military discipline was pervasive, it did not diminish Kamehameha's lively spirit of campus activities and innovative programs.

Below: *President Harold Kent and William Quinn, the first elected governor of Hawai'i, reviewing the Kamehameha troops at Mawaena Field in May, 1959.*

Left: *The Boys' School Armory in the late 1950s and early 1960s was well stocked with Army-issued weapons.*

Right: *"Ever Onward" is the translation of PI'IMUA on this medallion, designed by Colonel Harold Kent, and awarded to families of Kamehameha students lost in battle during WW II and the Korean War.*

57

At Kamehameha Schools the dress codes were strict—boys were required to be in uniform and girls' hemlines remained below the knee. No young lady would dare wear makeup or lipstick. And the campuses remained divided between the sexes with some awkward mixed dances. But the students were rarely bored since sports, recreation, music, ceremony and special cultural activities were always available and encouraged. Campus life was far more than drills, study and demerits.

One of the more unique opportunities for the boys and girls was the Bishop Museum program initiated by long-time teacher Donald Kilolani Mitchell. Eager that young students become acquainted with their Hawaiian culture while learning practical museum skills, Mitchell began the program in 1952.

Above: Students helped remodel the Kahili Room in the Bernice Pauahi Bishop Museum in 1953 as part of their work-study program.

Left: Students moved all of the ali'i portraits to the entrance of Bishop Hall for an exhibit. Photo circa 1958.

Above: Austin Kaawaloa, Class of 1956, demonstrating the use of an ancient Hawaiian drill. He participated in the Museum's living display in 1954.

Right: Kekoa Kaapu, Class of 1954, clad in authentic Hawaiian garb, stood at the entrance to a Bishop Museum exhibit, informing visitors about the various emblems of Hawaiian royalty.

Under Mitchell's supervision, sophomore and junior boys and girls worked at Bishop Museum at a variety of tasks for two periods in the morning or for an entire afternoon. Students served as docents, receptionists and guides or assisted in the library and laboratory sorting, indexing, and storing scientific specimens. In the process, these young people learned first-hand about their culture and history while making various Hawaiian crafts.

When the program finally ended ten years later, scores of students had served as museum docents and been given the unique opportunity to share their knowledge of their culture with the younger children of Hawai'i.

EMBLEMS OF ROYALTY IN OLD HAWAII

Members of the Class of 1955
(left to right): Winona Ahio,
Clifford Jamile, Marilyn Chu,
Clifford Carpenter, Odetta Mills
and William Greig.

Founder's Day Pledge

We, the pupils of the Kamehameha Schools,
In honor of the memory of our Aliʻi,
Pledge ourselves for the coming year
To strive to put from us such thoughts and feelings
As may tend to degrade our minds and bodies,
To give more time and strength
To gain all she wished us to gain,
And to strive to honor her name wherever we may be;
And we do this
That we may better prepare ourselves
To have such homes,
And such conditions
As shall tend to keep and develop for our race,
All those noble traits of character she possessed.

Uldrick Thompson
Teacher and Principal
of the School for Boys, 1898–1901

The firsthand learning experiences offered through the Bishop Museum program were characteristic of many of the Schools' vocational programs. Students who chose a technical curriculum began taking courses in agriculture, bookbinding, electricity, printing, auto mechanics, electronics, welding, wood carving, drafting or machine in the ninth grade. By the eleventh and twelfth grades, the "tech" cadets spent most of their time in "shop" while college-bound students gained credit in math, science or foreign language. Students spent one day of their school week working in the community or school as part of the Work Program introduced by President Kent.

Right: *Seventh graders from the Class of 1959 observing instructor Fritz Abplanalp's technique as he sculpts a face from wood. A world-renowned craftsman, Abplanalp taught students to make everything from simple furniture to award-winning sculptures.*

Right: *Stanley Merseberg, Class of 1957, holding two candidates for the Schools' Thanksgiving feast. Boys in agriculture classes raised chickens and turkeys and produced a limited amount of fresh vegetables and eggs for school use, which helped defray operating costs.*

Above: *William Davis and Alvin Johnson, Class of 1953, learned welding in the Schools' foundry as part of their vocational instruction.*

Left: *George Lincoln, Class of 1955, working at the machine shop.*

Right: *Music instructor Harold Turney directing the Boys' Glee Club at their 1954 Spring Concert in the Schools' auditorium. Kamehameha students produced two recordings of favorite songs in the 1950s.*

Above: *Vice Principal Howard Benham, Class of 1944, helping Mō'ī team member Carl Puhi, Class of 1954, with his equipment for a hui or intramural football game. Hui games allowed day and boarding students to learn the value of sportsmanship and team effort.*

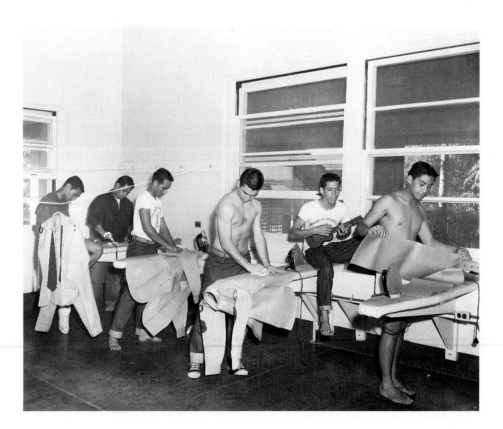

Right: *Boys in Kapuāiwa dormitory ironing their uniforms for inspection. Stressing self-reliance, boarders were expected to wash and iron their own clothes. Photo circa 1957.*

Right: *The silver citizenship pin was awarded to boys who received no more than 10 demerits and no more than three C's in attitude ratings.*

Below: *Kamehameha boys in 1954 continued the tradition of raising a metal cross at Punchbowl Cemetery as a community service. The cross was made in the 1930s by Kamehameha metal shop students.*

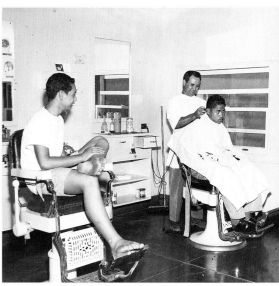

Above: *In the 1950s, students didn't need to go far for a regulation haircut. Barber Valentine Coelho giving Class of 1956 student Earl Umuiwi a trim while Douglas Guerrero looks on at the Schools' barber shop in 'Iolani dormitory.*

Left: *Robert Mossman,
Class of 1956, practicing
his volleys on the
Schools' tennis courts.*

If the Work Program didn't keep them busy, students always had the playing field. Sports were always popular at Kamehameha as the Warriors were active in football, basketball, track and field, cross country, volleyball, swimming, tennis, softball, baseball and riflery. Intramural or *Hui* sports including gymnastics, trampoline, archery and bowling were also favored by many students. Individual Warriors and Warriorettes were frequently recognized on the biweekly sports page of *Ka Mōʻī* along with the latest ILH and inter-*hui* news.

Right: *Student divers Melvin
Chun (top) and Kekoa Kaapu
practicing at Farrington High
School pool in 1953.
Kamehameha's pool was not
completed until 1964.*

Left: Both junior and senior varsity football games were well attended. No. 15, Ronald Kaanehe, Class of 1960, runs wild for the JV Warriors.

Below: In the 1950s, Kamehameha's baseball team played their Interscholastic games at the Honolulu Stadium in Mōʻiliʻili.

Right: *Roman Chai, Howard Lua and Apatai Akau* (left to right) *hiked into the forest above the campus to gather ti leaves for the 1954 Hoʻolauleʻa celebration.*

Another source of pride in achievement was offered through the annual spring *Hoʻolauleʻa*—an open house for students, parents, alumni and the general public. President Kent always extended a special invitation to this event to Island leaders and all public and private school principals. During the fifties, an annual average of nearly 3,000 visitors enjoyed exhibits of student photographs or artwork and the entertainment by JROTC drill teams, glee clubs, Hawaiian clubs, and P.E. classes. The day-long *Hoʻolauleʻa* activities included movies showing highlights of football games as well as class displays in the shops, home economics and science classes. Capping the activities was a major *lūʻau* prepared by the students. Boys and girls had time off from school to gather ti leaves and prepare the *lau lau* for the all-day festival.

Hoʻolauleʻa represented a gathering of the Kamehameha family in which students, parents and alumni took great pride. "Our life was really special," remembers Mrs. Stender of these days. "We were like one happy family."

Above: *Melvin Wong, Class of 1958, demonstrating how to bone a ti leaf.*

Right: *Emily Wilson, Hawley Burningham, and Mary Puaa prepare some of the thousands of lau lau that were required to feed the crowds that came to the 1953 Hoʻolauleʻa.*

Left: Henry Kaahea and Jerald Chong, Class of 1959, displayed their volcano project during the 1958 Hoʻolauleʻa.

Below: Student performances took place in front of Pākī Hall (now called Keōua). The audience for these pageants during the 1950s was often over 3,000 people.

Below: *In 1954, students sailed from Honolulu to Nawiliwili Harbor in Kaua'i aboard the yacht Manuiwa, which was a gift to the Schools from Harold Dillingham. Navigation classes were taught for two years before the yacht was sold in 1955.*

Above: *Kekūhaupi'o was transformed into King Neptune's underwater palace for the 1954 Junior-Senior Prom. Students attended mandatory dance lessons so they were well prepared for class dances.*

Below: *Graduation day, 1955. Kekūhaupi'o field house, once an airplane hangar, was the center of campus activities in the 1950s. Sporting events, proms, Founder's Day ceremonies, Song Contests and graduations were held there.*

Left: On October 6, 1953, the Schools' radio station KVOK (Voice of Kamehameha) aired its inaugural broadcast. Hawai'i's first FM station at 88.1 on the dial, KVOK entertained audiences in the studio and at home with musical selections by the Girls' Glee Club.

Below: Boarders often competed for prizes for the best table decorations at special holiday dinners. The winners of the 1954 May Day prize celebrate their victory.

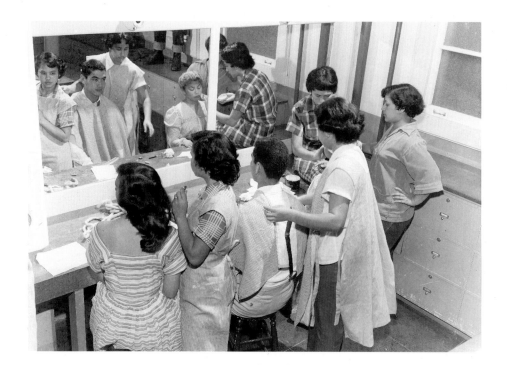

Left: *Students getting ready for the Senior play in 1954. Talent shows and one-act plays were staged in the Auditorium in the 1940s and 1950s.*

Below: *Girls School students marching to Mawaena Field to participate in the All School Parade held at the end of the academic year. Photo circa 1953.*

It would be impossible to separate memories of growing up from the days spent in Senior Cottage changing diapers or those long, sweaty hours on the JROTC drill field. How many nights were spent in those teenage dormitory discussions of world-shattering importance, wondering who will ask whom to dance at the Saturday social? How many nights were spent studying after "lights out" in the bathroom or under blankets with flashlights?

The special events would become the most unforgettable—the laughter, tears and pride of the Song Contests. Or that day when youth and innocence were at last set aside— graduation.

Left: *Weekend hikes and leisure walks often took place in and around the beautifully landscaped grounds of Kekāuluohi girls' dormitory on the upper campus.*

Below: *Trustee George M. Collins presented diplomas to 85 boys and 69 girls at the Class of 1956 graduation held in Kekūhaupiʻo.*

On March 12, 1959 Hawai'i also set aside its youth and innocence. For some Islanders, statehood was a recognition of Hawai'i's full adulthood into the United States. On the Kamehameha Schools campus, the mood was festive. *Ke Ali'i Pauahi*, the school newsletter, described "a jubilant serpentine of students from the two upper schools, headed by the JROTC band," as they marched from their campuses to Kekūhaupi'o for an assembly. They were greeted by the Prepsters and addressed by President Kent and Trustee Frank Midkiff. JROTC boys fired a triumphant twenty-one gun salute.

Hawai'i had now become an equal member in modern America. With that distinction would come new, surprising forces of change that would require Kamehameha Schools to steer a steady course through the next, sometimes turbulent decade.

Left: *Statehood for Hawai'i! Kamehameha seniors marched from 'Iolani Palace to Kawaiaha'o Church in March, 1959, where they sang in the statehood celebration program.*

Above: *Kamehameha's 1918 championship football team poses for a yearbook photo.*

Left: *A player for the Kamehameha girl's softball team winds up for a strikeout pitch in 1982.*

I mua Kamehameha!

I mua Kamehameha! Forward Kamehameha! Ever striving for victory! This rallying cheer that was also the battle cry of the warrior king for whom the School is named, has given special inspiration to Kamehameha athletes and supporters for many decades.

From the earliest days when the young men carried the pigskin over the rocky, dusty playfield of the Pālama campus, to modern times when Kamehameha's girls' softball team captured the 1987 state championship, the Warriors have consistently been outstanding athletes.

On the field, in the gymnasium or in the pool, Kamehameha athletes have always competed vigorously and skillfully. They have strengthened body, mind and character while upholding the ideals of good sportsmanship, self-discipline and teamwork.

"I mua Kamehameha"

I mua Kamehameha e, A lanakila 'oe,
Paio, paio like mau, I ola kou inoa,
Ka wā nei hō'ike a 'e 'oe, 'A'ohe lua ou,
E lawe lilo ka ha'aheo no Kamehameha e.

Forward Kamehameha, Until you have gained the victory,
Go forward, strive in unity, That your name may live.
Go forward, This is the time for you to reveal (show),
Take the victory with pride for Kamehameha.

by Charles E. King
Class of 1891

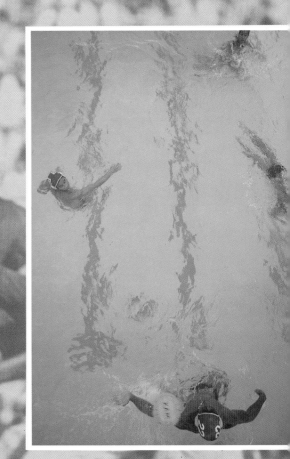

Above: *Water polo players in Ke'elikōlani pool in 1982.*

Left: *Tension, anxiety and determination are captured in the expressions of 1954 Kamehameha basketball player Ernest Chan.*

Above: *Kamehameha's 1940 basketball stars.*

Above: *A 1950 basketball player models the official uniform of the day.*

Below: *Kamehameha hurdlers compete in a track meet at 'Iolani School in 1964.*

Above: An ILH official signals a touchdown at an
Aloha Stadium game in 1983.

Left: Bowling became a popular
sport for boys and girls in the 1950s.
Fannie Kealoha displays top form
in this 1957 photo taken at
Kamehameha Bowl located just
below the School's campus.

Kamehameha ROTC cadets Danny Rice, Pat Spencer, Kenneth Ching, Walter Ritte and Steven Davis proudly pose in front of the nation's Capitol during their visit to march in John F. Kennedy's presidential inaugural parade in 1961.

Chapter IV
Challenges at the Campus Gate

The Sixties

January 20, 1961 was a very special day for one hundred Kamehameha Schools' JROTC cadets fighting the cold weather in Washington, D.C. The students, members of the band, color guard and battle group, had been chosen to represent Hawai'i in the inaugural parade for President John F. Kennedy. For many of these young Hawaiians, this trip to Washington was their first mainland experience. With a spirit of awe and adventure, they visited national monuments, toured the United States Capitol and fought their first snowball fight. Most importantly, as they carried the flags of their nation and state in the presidential parade, they demonstrated to the world that "Americanism is a matter of mind and heart; Americanism is not, and never was, a matter of race or ancestry."

Being recognized as first-class Americans was important to Kamehameha students as the decade of the sixties commenced. Hawai'i had become the fiftieth state and young Hawaiian men and women took pride in their new national status. They were also proud of their school as Kamehameha celebrated its seventy-fifth year in 1962–63.

Below: *Lei-bedecked cadets and their ROTC instructors pause for a final group photo before boarding the plane that will carry them to new experiences in Washington, D.C.*

"It was while we were at the Capitol that it began to snow! Can you imagine the sight we presented: ninety Hawaiian boys having a snow fight?"

Jan Dill
Class of 1961

Below: *A tour of the White House was one of the highlights of the Washington, D.C. visit.*

Above: *Shoveling ice, throwing snowballs and fighting the chill were new experiences for these Hawaiian young men, many of whom had never before seen snow.*

Above: *ROTC cadet Mike Chun, Class of 1961, is greeted in Washington, D.C. by Hawai'i senator Hiram Fong.*

Left: *The cadets discovered their American heritage through visits to museums, monuments, memorials and historic sites.*

The Diamond Jubilee festivities were extensive. The Glee Club produced a special album of Hawaiian music; a mammoth *lūʻau* was held on the campus; and the Honolulu newspapers published a special edition on Bernice Pauahi Bishop and the Schools. The Schools also sponsored a series of lectures featuring fifteen outstanding scholars of Hawaiian studies. The lectures were later published by the Kamehameha Schools Press as *Aspects of Hawaiian Life and Environment*, a work that has become an important reference for educators, researchers, and others interested in Hawaiian culture.

April Peeples Chock, Class of 1953, performs a spirited hula ʻauana at the Diamond Jubilee lūʻau.

The mood was upbeat as teachers, students and staff looked forward to a decade of growth, progressive education and success in applying acquired knowledge and skills. Few, however, could have envisioned the transformation of academic and social life that was soon to take place.

Left: Emily Kekaula Taylor (left), Class of 1915; Edwin P. Murray, Class of 1909; and Louise Aoe Wongkong McGregor, Class of 1897; reminisce about their student days at the Alumni Reunion lū'au in 1962. Murray served as a Kamehameha Trustee from 1940 to 1968.

Below: The Diamond Jubilee lū'au was a mammoth affair with generations of graduates crowding Kekūhaupi'o gymnasium to share an evening of entertainment, good food and special memories.

For seventy-five years, Kamehameha Schools had sought to educate Hawaiian youth so that they could compete in a changing Island society. Statehood accelerated those changes during the sixties as Hawaiʻi's population expanded and tourism became the foremost industry. If native Hawaiians were to fully participate in this "new" Hawaiʻi, then improved and more varied educational opportunities would be vital. Recognizing the Schools' need to reassess its programs, the Trustees in 1961 hired the consultant team of Booz, Allen and Hamilton to conduct an extensive analysis of Kamehameha and recommend how to improve its services.

Below: *From traditional Hawaiian craft to contemporary sculpture and design, the Student Art Exhibit showcased the talent of students from kindergarten to grade twelve.*

When the Booz, Allen and Hamilton study was completed, their recommendations offered a daring, new vision for Kamehameha. Emphasizing the Schools' mission to develop "the minds, bodies and Protestant Christian values of young people, especially those of Hawaiian ancestry," the report suggested innovations in three areas: campus instruction, extension education, and scholarships.

Campus instruction was to be given the highest priority as the Preparatory Department and secondary schools were advised to broaden the range of educational experiences. Students who were college-bound should be given a solid academic background, while vocational students should receive high quality training for gainful employment.

Extension education was a revolutionary concept for Kamehameha Schools. Through cooperation with other institutions such as the Department of Education and Bishop Museum, the Schools were advised to initiate off-campus

programs for communities with large numbers of young Hawaiians. Classes were to be offered in reading, writing and speech, as well as Hawaiian culture studies and special summer activities. Counseling services and special educational assistance programs were also to be made available.

The scholarship program was recommended so that outstanding Hawaiian youth would be encouraged to continue their post-high school education. Young people with potential were to be placed in positions of leadership, supported in their college goals or encouraged in useful employment at technical and lower management levels.

These challenges posed by the Booz, Allen and Hamilton study were met by President James Bushong who replaced Colonel Harold Kent after his retirement in 1963. The new administration put emphasis on campus instruction as efforts were made to improve the teaching staff and upgrade the curriculum.

Above: *Seniors Momi Ho, Aaron Akaka and Le Van Sequeira admire the craftsmanship of a student's koa bowl at the Diamond Jubilee Student Art Exhibit.*

Above: *In 1962, KSB junior Barry Wood won a school-wide competition for an ROTC shoulder patch design commemorating Kamehameha's 75th Anniversary. The special patches were distributed to all cadets to be worn on their uniforms throughout the 1962–63 school year.*

Above: *Kamehameha students reached for
the stars when the Bishop Museum opened
its new planetarium in the early 1960s.*

Right: *Mealtimes, preceded by grace
sung in Hawaiian, were opportunities for
Kamehameha students to practice good
table manners and polite conversation while
enjoying nutritious food in a family-style
dining atmosphere.*

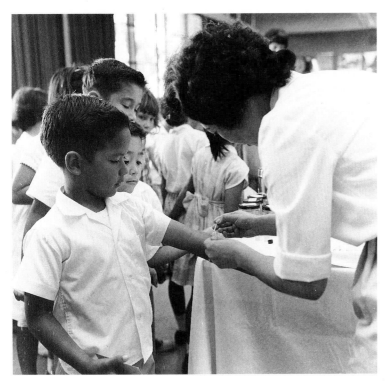

Above: *Kamehameha provided its students with outstanding medical and dental care. However, nothing was dreaded more by students than waiting in line for polio and tuberculosis vaccinations.*

The Preparatory Department continued an effective program of elementary education in the sixties. Children were not only given fundamental reading, writing and math skills, but were provided with sound Christian values, manners and a strong sense of their ethnic heritage.

Miss Caroline Curtis, revered storyteller to a generation of Kamehameha Prepsters, was especially memorable. As entertainer Brickwood Galuteria, Class of 1973, says "I'll never forget the legend she shared with us about how Maui harnessed the sun. I still recall it whenever I'm trying to overcome a difficult task."

Another popular activity was the annual *Makahiki* celebration. Dressed in *malo* and *kīkepa*, fourth graders took the lead roles in the re-enactment of the Hawaiian season of peace, religious festivities and gift-giving to the god, Lono. They played the ancient games of *ulu maika* and *moa pahe'e* and presented fresh fruit and vegetables, dried fish and canned goods wrapped in ti leaves or *tapa*, to the *Makahiki* chief and chiefess. The canned goods were later given by the students to the elderly Hawaiians at Lunalilo Home. They also performed songs and dances for the *kūpuna* in an encounter that one alumni says "gave you a good feeling to think that you might have brightened their day."

Left: *Art teacher Lois Horne helps Class of 1977 students create mosaic tile designs that would eventually hang in the school office, library or on outside walls.*

89

Haunani Oliveira, Class of 1974, strings a lei in preparation for a school pageant.

Above: A sense of heritage was perpetuated through the annual enactment of the Makahiki festival, presided over by the image of Lono, god of peace and agriculture. After the ceremonies, the hoʻokupu of canned goods, fruits or flowers would be shared with the kupuna at Lunalilo Home.

Left: Respect and gratitude were instilled in Kamehameha students through the tradition of honoring the Schools' founder, Bernice Pauahi Bishop, and her husband Charles Reed Bishop.

Above: Prom nights were memorable occasions for formal gowns, corsages and "dress blues." Teanini Rosha, Class of 1962, and Cedric Ludington, Class of 1961, greet School for Boys principal Allen Bailey and Mrs. Bailey in the receiving line.

Right: Senior Chester Mahelona wore traditional Hawaiian garments during his installment as student body president for the 1962–63 year. Lambert Hiram, Class of 1964, and James Hussey, Class of 1963, look on during the ceremony held at Mawaena field.

At the secondary schools, Kamehameha students were encouraged to prepare themselves for higher education. Under the guidance of Gladys Ainoa Brandt at the School for Girls, the first Hawaiian principal at Kamehameha, and Allen Bailey at the School for Boys, the college preparatory program was expanded in the areas of foreign language and business education. Honor students were also offered accelerated courses in English, math and social studies.

Improved and expanded facilities on the Kapālama Heights campus enriched the students' learning environment. Construction during the sixties began with Pākī Hall, a three-story, twenty-eight room building on the School for Boys campus designed by Class of 1919 alumnus Ted Vierra. The Bernice Pauahi Bishop Administration building and the Princess Ruth Keʻelikōlani swimming pool soon followed. Kamāmalu, finished in 1966, was a modern, imaginatively conceived three-story structure housing the elementary office, library, ten classrooms, a band and orchestra room and an art studio.

Below: *Up until 1967, each Kamehameha senior girl spent six weeks boarding in Keōpuōlani Senior Cottage where she learned basic household and child care skills. Wilhelmina Atai, Sherol Lum and Diane Medina, all members of the Class of 1962, show off their infant charges.*

Above: "Being a part of the 'Hawaiianess' of Kamehameha was thrilling," remembers Mike Pavich, Class of 1968. Aloha shirts and mu'umu'u were colorful reminders of that spirit.

These alterations at Kamehameha also extended to the tempo of campus life. Under the stewardship of Colonel Kent, rigorous military discipline dominated student behavior—long-sleeved uniforms, demerits and drills marked the daily routine.

In contrast, during the tenure of President Bushong, extensive student control was viewed as detrimental to self-reliance. The military tone of the campus was relaxed to an extent, as students were permitted to wear short-sleeved khaki uniforms, and aloha shirts and slacks on Fridays. Training in discipline and neatness was maintained in a more comfortable setting.

The change in long-standing traditions was perhaps most dramatic as Kamehameha Schools ended seventy-five years of campus segregation based on gender. In the fall of 1965, the faculties of the School for Boys and School for Girls merged and relocated so that each department (English, math, social studies and science) was situated on only one campus. This change not only permitted fluctuation in class size and greater opportunities for team teaching and individualized instruction, it also provided a more realistic educational setting.

Initially, the new organization did not alter the autonomous nature of the two schools—boys and girls were still under the supervision of their respective principals.

Left: *Blase Lee Loy and Allene Wong, Class of 1967, ponder a vector diagram in a Pākī classroom.*

Below: *The emphasis on excellence in academics resulted in the creation of honors classes in various subjects and independent study seminars.*

Coeducation was enthusiastically embraced by the majority of pupils. Of course there were some apprehensions—gone were the days when girls and boys only *talked* about the opposite sex, but didn't have to worry about how they *acted* around them. Also gone were the ninth grade mandatory dance lessons which one alumni remembers as "simply awful." Lacking both self-assurance and experience, a line of sweaty-palmed young boys used to form on one side of the gym looking nervously at the equally uncomfortable line of fidgeting girls on the other side. Coeducation eventually put both sides a little more at ease.

In the midst of these challenges, one aspect of life at Kamehameha Schools remained constant. The excitement of activity, the joy of school pride and the thrill of competition continued to offer students the "best years of their lives."

Above: Kamehameha "beauties" kick-up their heels at an annual United Fund Drive talent show during the 1961–62 school year.

Right: Ralph Niau, Class of 1968, and his guest enjoy the military formality and protocol of the annual ROTC ball.

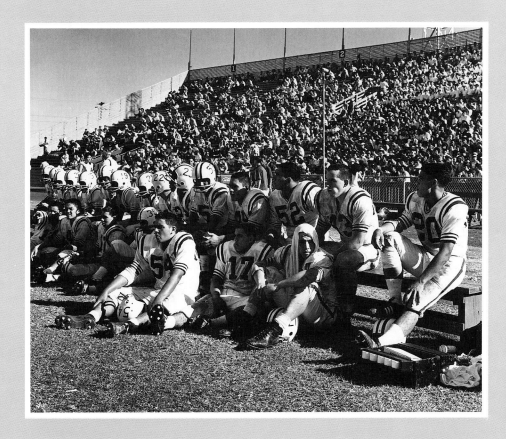

Left: *The 1961–62 Warriors watch their teammates on the Honolulu Stadium field in Mōʻiliʻili.*

Below: *Kamehameha entered a floral float in the 1961 Aloha Week parade.*

The sixties are usually remembered as years of rebellion for American youth nationwide who questioned the authority and values of their leaders, teachers, ministers and parents. Losing faith in their nation, they turned to outward acts of protest which were manifested in the length of their hair or style of life. At Kamehameha, the majority of students possessed respect for their parents and loyalty to their school that softened much of the impact of that youthful frustration.

Right: *Returning after spring break or summer vacation, Kamehameha boarders looked forward to renewing friendships and getting back into the "swing" of dormitory life.*

Below: *Moral values were instilled in Kamehameha students through devotional services, Christian education and the recitation of hymns and psalms. Bishop Memorial Church services were held on Sundays in the auditorium.*

Below: *Boarder Stephen Park, Class of 1964, enjoys the afternoon sun while he studies outside the dormitories.*

Campus life was marked more by productivity and camaraderie than political protests. Since many students were boarders, dormitory parties, dances, study sessions and long hours of "talk story" occupied much of their free time. Sports also remained popular—especially football. The Warriors had perhaps their most glorious season on the gridiron in 1960. Coach Calvin Chai took honors as Coach of the Year as his team triumphed in the Interscholastic League with seven victories and only one defeat.

The *Honolulu Advertiser* selected an unprecedented five Kamehameha School football players for the All-Star team of the year, including Anthony Ah Yat (Center), Leroy Kuamoo (Guard), Agenhart Ellis (Tackle), Michael Chun (End), and Kamehameha's "breakaway threat," the league's leading scorer Sargeant Napuunoa (Half-back). Later stars such as Rockne Freitas and Sam Harris would carry on this winning spirit of the Warriors.

When the new olympic-size swimming pool was completed in 1964, students quickly took advantage of water sports. The pool, named Keʻelikōlani in honor of Mrs. Bishop's cousin, Princess Ruth, was an impressive 50-meter, 8-lane plunge that was constantly used by the students. "The swim club was my life at Kameha-meha," says swim club alumnus Haunani Oliveira Tsuji, Class of 1974. With other swimmers, she began participating in water sports in the first grade and continued through her junior year.

Under coaches such as Sonny Tanabe, Woolsey Rice, Ed DeSilva, and Bill Smith, daily practice began before breakfast at 5:30 a.m. and again from 4:00 to 6:00 p.m. in the afternoon. The swim club members were so dedicated, that their morning practice sometimes lasted through morning meals. A box of cereal downed while showering or on the run to the first morning class was "breakfast" for some. The team spent so much time together they formed an ʻohana, and team parents became "uncles and aunties."

Kamehameha's long-awaited olympic pool opened in 1964, providing students with an outstanding on-campus swimming facility. The 50-meter, 8-lane pool was named after Mrs. Bishop's cousin, Princess Ruth Keʻelikōlani.

Left: *At Kamehameha, girls were as active as boys in all types of sports. Photo 1968–69.*

Below: *Kamehameha and Punahou were classic rivals in team and individual sports such as wrestling. Photo 1964–65.*

In some cases, student activities reached well beyond campus. Through a mainland exchange program, a few Kamehameha students were given the opportunity to spend a year in the continental United States. In 1965, four students exchanged places with mainland high school juniors, thus experiencing their home and school lifestyles. In turn, the mainland students moved into Kamehameha's multi-cultural environment. This annual exchange continued into the 1970s.

The sixties were also remembered for the Kamehameha carnival. Initiated as a fund-raising event in 1943, carnivals had traditionally been country farm fairs. The few thousand dollars generated by these early fairs were used for the Schools' Kōkua Fund which helped pay the costs of school supplies or clothing for students who would not otherwise be able to afford them. It also covered the publication of *Ke Aliʻi Pauahi*, the magazine sent to parents and graduates.

In 1964, the Parent-Teacher and Alumni Associations joined forces with the Schools to sponsor a much larger carnival which helped to more than quadruple profits. These larger events culminated in April 1968, when Kamehameha held its 25th annual carnival on Malalo field outside of Kekūhaupiʻo gymnasium. In addition to the rides, cotton candy and game booths, there was a dance, talent show, and a Hawaiian revue. Over $44,500 was raised with about $15,000 going to post-high school scholarships for graduates who wished to continue their education.

Above: *Bright lights, music, laughter and the smell of hot malasadas dominate the midway of the 1964–65 Carnival held on Kekūhaupiʻo field.*

Above: The Carnival was an opportunity for Class of 1965 students Patrick Mitchell, Charles Naumu, Hartwell Kaeo and Henry Akina to sell succulent squash, melon, corn and other fruits and vegetables at the produce booth.

Left: Nalei Kanoho, Jeanine Oana and Kauanoe Kamana, Class of 1969, loved every minute of their high-flying ride during the 1962–63 Carnival.

Above: *Class picnics provided a full day of fun in the surf, sun and sand. Class of 1962 members Leslie Von Arnswaldt (left with seaweed)* and *Ned Goodness cloak Kevin "Chubby" Mahoe in an itchy suit of seaweed on Kalama beach.*

Right: *Patrick O'Sullivan (with guitar), Class of 1962, leads his classmates in a song as they relax on the shady Kalama beach cottage lawn.*

Class picnics during the sixties created some special memories for students. Usually held at Kalama, a leased beach property in Kailua, the picnics were a celebration of school spirit and friendship. "Everything about it was great," remembers alumnus Tsuji, "from singing songs at the top of your lungs all the way down and back in the bus, eating the sand while trying to body surf on the waves in front of the beach cottage, to playing volleyball and throwing water balloons." It was a time to renew old friendships and make new ones as the entire grade level got together to enjoy the beach and surf.

Right: *Volleyball was a great picnic activity for everyone.*

Above: *Kimo Kahoano (back left), Mabelmae Kamahele, Walker Beamer and Sanders Makua take KP duty at the grill during their senior class picnic in 1966.*

Left: *Roy Alameda, Class of 1963, gets into the "spirit" at his class picnic as he passes an orange to a female classmate without using his hands.*

The conscientiousness of Kamehameha students in the sixties was best illustrated by their outstanding academic record. Among the three hundred and sixty-seven seniors of the Class of 1970, ninety earned honors and thirty-eight received highest honors. Standardized achievement tests that year showed that eighty percent of Kamehameha students scored above the national average in reading, math, science, language arts, social studies, listening and writing.

Cases of flagrant student dissent were isolated. "During this particularly difficult year which witnessed dissension, demonstrations and discord on high school campuses throughout our country," the Schools' 1970 annual report observed, "Kamehameha students and staff members conducted themselves in an exemplary manner."

Yet this decade of protest did not leave Kamehameha untouched. Some students began to question traditional values and the role of authority in school and society. Accepted standards and the status quo were re-examined, and as a result, the beginnings of cultural awareness and a sense of ethnic pride were stirred at Kamehameha. Being Hawaiian, students discovered, was a matter of spirit, a feeling that would eventually transform the Kamehameha Schools' experience.

Below: *While many mainland high school campuses suffered student unrest and dissent during the sixties, the majority of students on the Kamehameha campus occupied themselves with the important business of learning.*

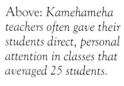

Above: *Kamehameha teachers often gave their students direct, personal attention in classes that averaged 25 students.*

Left: *English, the sciences and the humanities were emphasized at Kamehameha during the sixties as academic curriculum was up-graded and expanded. Members of the Class of 1967 (left to right): Barbara Benham, Stella Badua, Clara Jean Garcia and Peter Hanohano collaborate on a lab project.*

Right: *Kahealani Kaiama led the combined classes in the State's anthem, Hawai'i Pono'i at the 1986 Song Contest.*

Above: *Once the new Kapālama Heights campus opened, Song Contests were held in the auditorium on the Girl's School campus. Photo circa 1945.*

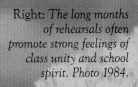

Right: *The long months of rehearsals often promote strong feelings of class unity and school spirit. Photo 1984.*

Kamehameha Sings!

Since the late 18th century when their *mele* or chant intermingled with Christian hymns and *haole* melodies, Hawaiians have composed and performed unique, lyrical compositions and dances. This musical embodiment of language and culture has always been important to Hawaiians: as a way to worship their ancient gods; as a means of communicating feelings and ideas; and as a way to share pleasure with one another.

The expression of music is still highly valued in modern Hawai'i, and is a significant part of being a student at Kamehameha. As long ago as November 1887, the strong, clear voices of nearly forty young Hawaiian men sang out for King Kalākaua and his royal entourage during the Schools' opening day ceremonies.

Thirty-three years later, Kamehameha's most popular musical event was born on the steps of Bishop Hall. Illuminated only by a circle of car headlights, one hundred twenty boys competed in the first Song Contest. By the 1930s, Song Contest had become so well-known, it was broadcast live on island radio. For the last two decades, the spectacular annual competition has been viewed by thousands of people around the state through live television coverage.

Each year parents, families, friends and music enthusiasts witness in one glorious night, the result of months of daily, dedicated practice and striving for perfection. But behind the anxious smiles and the hands clasped in nervous anticipation, invisible to the darkened audience, are deep feelings of camaraderie, accomplishment and elation.

When it is all over, winner embraces loser, senior salutes freshman, and all voices swell to the strains of the school song. Generation after generation of students take with them the special memory of Song Contest, and the richness that Hawaiian music adds to the soul.

Above: *In 1964, Song Contest outgrew Kekūhaupi'o and moved to the Neal Blaisdell Center where it continues to attract capacity crowds each year.*

Left: *Dramatic and authentic performances of hula kahiko by a select group of students have been popular Hō'ike features in recent years. Photo 1984.*

Above: *Hours of practice to perfect pitch, pronunciation and phrasing culminate in a few moments of glorious song. Photo 1986.*

Above: *1987 senior Iolani Kamau'u ecstatically accepts a broom from Trustee Richard Lyman, knowing that it signifies his class has swept top honors in all three contest categories.*

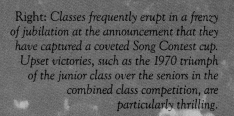

Right: *Classes frequently erupt in a frenzy of jubilation at the announcement that they have captured a coveted Song Contest cup. Upset victories, such as the 1970 triumph of the junior class over the seniors in the combined class competition, are particularly thrilling.*

Above: *Senior class song leaders and presidents Yvonne Reese, Joy Ahn, Rodney Kalua and Simeon Akaka pose with their trophies following the March 1956 contest.*

Above: *1984 song leaders Isaiah Jeremiah, Kawika Freitas and Kalua Leong are laden with the floral expressions of their peers' and families' pride.*

Left: *"There are few places where you could get some 2,000 teenagers to cooperate so well on a project that receives so much public exposure as Song Contest," commented Kamehameha Director of Campus Programs Robert Springer.*

Hawaiian dance is one way in which Kamehameha students express the rejuvenation of pride in their heritage.

Chapter V
The Vision Burns Bright
The Seventies and Eighties

Ka poʻe kahiko, the people of old, once lived in the *ahupuaʻa* of Kapālama. They harvested *ʻuala, uhi* and *kalo* from terraced fields, imparting to new generations the skill to nurture the land. They witnessed the cycles of life from birth to maturity to death which they immortalized in legend, dance and chant. They worshipped their gods, respected their chiefs and sought harmony with the mysteries of life.

More than two hundred years later, the spirit of *ka poʻe kahiko* has found renewal and veneration among a modern generation of Hawaiians on the slopes of that ancient *ahupuaʻa.* In language, poetry, legend, music, dance, art, crafts and spiritual knowledge, Kamehameha students were eager to discover the significance of their past while preparing to succeed in modern Hawaiʻi.

The Schools' leadership of the seventies and eighties was ready to foster this revived ethnic pride. Jack Darvill was selected by the Trustees to replace President James Bushong in 1971. He and other individuals such as Tom Hamilton and Robert Springer were committed to perpetuating Kamehameha as an educational leader in the Hawaiian community and the state.

Below: *Jack Darvill became President of the Kamehameha Schools in 1972 and encouraged the perpetuation of Hawaiian culture and the expansion of services beyond the campus.*

Right: *Intermediate students Lina Naipo, Camilynn Mahelona, and Donna Mae Heath fashion haku lei for a May Day celebration in 1986.*

Below: *Campus life includes many opportunities for socializing and having fun. Photo 1980.*

Early in Darvill's presidency, the Schools began to broaden its contacts in the community and strengthen its ties with other organizations which benefitted Hawaiians. The Department of Hawaiian Home Lands, Queen Lili'uokalani Children's Center and Lunalilo Home joined Kamehameha to form HSIA, Hawaiian Services, Institutions and Agencies, to coordinate services to the Hawaiian community.

Public response was sought, as a community advisory committee recommended that the Schools' administration "do more for more of Hawai'i's youth, particularly Hawaiian young people with special educational needs; help them to integrate into the mainstream of American society, yet retain a sense of their own identity, an awareness of their culture."

Hawaiian youth would benefit from Kamehameha's full range of resources to develop their "highest potential as effective participants in contemporary society." The vision of Princess Pauahi, born nearly a hundred years before, continued to guide the Trustees through this era of growth.

Above: *In the 1980s, students like Wendy Thompson can take advantage of opportunities that help them reach their highest potential while retaining a sense of their cultural identity. Photo 1983.*

Left: *Modern classroom environments foster positive attitudes about learning.*

115

By the seventies, Kamehameha was widely recognized as one of Hawai'i's finest educational institutions, providing students with a sense of their heritage, and the opportunity to master the skills necessary to succeed.

From admission through graduation, students were to be given personal attention through comprehensive student services. Support was offered in the form of financial aid, boarding assistance, health services, career guidance and religious counseling.

New facilities also helped teachers and students attain a high level of excellence. The Frank E. Midkiff Learning Center, completed in 1977, included a library that could shelve 75,000 books, a complete television studio, graphic arts and audio-visual departments, a student production center and a special Hawaiiana room.

Kamehameha increasingly emphasized a college preparatory curriculum, and at the request of the student government, an honors program was initiated. "Honors courses," Sammiedean James, Class of 1986, recalls, "were more challenging than regular classes and allowed me to sample the demands of a college curriculum before I actually enrolled in college."

Above: Students Betsy Benham, Corbett Roy, Rowena Lau, and Orlando Orphilla posed for this portrait with Trustee Frank E. Midkiff in 1976.

Right: The Midkiff Learning Center's Hawaiian Studies room contains one of the State's best collections of books, photographs, news clippings and scrapbooks on Polynesian topics. Photo 1983.

116

Left: *Kamehameha students receive individualized attention from the School's staff of competent, caring teachers.*

Above: *Computer use has become common in many campus classrooms. Students are introduced to computer studies beginning in kindergarten. Photo 1986.*

Left: *Students in television classes learn about aspects of video production utilizing the learning center's modern, fully equipped television studio. Photo circa 1980.*

In 1973, ROTC, a long-standing tradition at Kamehameha, went from a full four-year to a two-year program. The change was especially evident in the boys' attire. Although dress codes and grooming standards remained conservative, ROTC uniforms were only worn on drill days.

In place of the boys' ROTC requirement and home economics for the girls, Hawaiian language and culture, formerly elective courses, were added to the high school graduation requirements. More elective classes were offered.

Notes Anthony Ramos, Class of 1958, who became secondary school principal in 1977, "There have been trade-offs. Emphasis today is on personal and academic self-discipline instead of the stringent military discipline of the four-year ROTC program. We offer a stronger college prep program and it's paying off in the number of students who pursue a post-high school education. Today, more than 85% of our seniors indicate they will continue their education after graduation."

As the campus curriculum continued to be developed and refined, Kamehameha prepared to offer educational opportunities to Hawaiian students in the community. An expansive series of language skills instruction, summer extension classes and public activities to promote Hawaiian language, culture, history and values was initiated. The impact of these extension programs was to be dynamic and far-reaching.

Right: ROTC changed in the 1970s from a full four-year program to a two-year required course with an additional two years as an elective.

Left: *Most Kamehameha students in the 1980s prepare for challenging post-high school educational experiences. Photo 1985.*

Above: *Lifelong physical fitness is now the goal of Kamehameha's P.E. programs. Photo 1982.*

Left: *Members of the orchestra are often called upon to perform at special events on campus and in the community. Photo 1985.*

Above: *Summer Explorers learn about Hawaiian culture through classes in Hawaiian language, music, dance, arts and crafts, and games. Photo 1982.*

Kamehameha's ambitious extension of services was well underway by the mid-seventies. Twenty-eight separate activities benefitted a wide range of the Hawaiian community: a mother in Hau'ula learning to play creative games with her six-month-old infant; a 10-year-old sanding his *ipu* to use in *hula* class; or a grandmother earning her high school diploma at evening classes.

Although the concept of extension services had been introduced in the 1961 Booz, Allen and Hamilton report, efforts to implement programs were modest. Summer extension centers in rural O'ahu and the neighbor islands operated from 1963 to 1967, and laid the foundation for cooperation between Kamehameha and the Department of Education that would be critical to the future success of the Schools' extension and research programs.

Two of the earliest and most successful extension programs were begun in 1968, as Kamehameha actively sought to take its teachers, resources and knowledge beyond the confines of the campus to the community.

"Explorations" and "Nā Pono Hawai'i" emphasized the sharing of Hawaiian cultural materials in an educational setting. Explorations is a week-long summer program open to fifth grade Hawaiian children. The boys and girls participated in an intensive study of Hawaiian history and culture through classes in Hawaiian language, music, dance, crafts, games and field trips.

Right: *Canoe paddling is a popular Explorations activity. Photo 1985.*

"*Thank you so very much for having my son as a participant in Explorations '86. He came home singing the songs he learned, and very excited at having learned so much about his Hawaiian culture.*"

Parent of a Student enrolled in
Explorations Program in 1986

Above: Over the past ten years, hundreds of acres of Bishop Estate land on the island of Hawai'i have been planted with native koa. Extension Education Director Fred Cachola, Class of 1953, and Land Manager William Rosehill, Class of 1968, watch as Trustee Richard Lyman checks on a koa sapling's growth.

Right: Summer Extension Education students test themselves on their newly acquired knowledge of Hawaiian studies. Photo 1982.

Nā Pono Hawaiʻi was a team of resource specialists that visited public and private schools throughout the islands. They introduced teachers and students to various aspects of Hawaiian culture through lectures, demonstrations and displays of artifacts.

The success of these two programs and the desire to offer more led to the hiring of a fulltime director of Extension Education.

In 1971, under Fred Cachola, Class of 1953, the size and scope of the extension programs changed dramatically. "More for Hawaiian children" became the motto of the Extension Education Division. Kamehameha began working with the Department of Education and Hawaiian community activists to help Hawaiian youngsters. The early seventies were a time of searching and risk-taking because the Schools needed to establish credibility in the community.

Within five years, Kamehameha's outreach included alternative learning centers, support for the revival of Hawaiian culture and language, and post-high school scholarship assistance. And, for the first time, some of the community-based projects were located on land owned by Kamehameha.

Pauahi's legacy went far beyond the campus. Alienated teenagers at Hōnaunau applied math concepts to making a fish-drying box, and Kamehameha tutors helped elementary students in Papakōlea improve their reading skills by two grade levels.

Above: *Nā Hoʻokama a Pauahi (Adopted Children of Pauahi) scholarships enable non-Kamehameha Hawaiian young people to pursue post-high school educational activities. Photo 1983.*

Below: *Kamehameha works with the Department of Education to develop alternative education programs such as the Hale O Hoʻoponopono project on the island of Hawaiʻi. Photo 1981.*

Kamehameha Summer Programs offer a wide range of educational and recreational experiences to students in grades K–11 statewide. Photo 1986.

Left: *Summer school programs are also held on neighbor islands in cooperation with the State Department of Education. Photo 1984.*

Below: *Kaua'i youngsters hike through a lo'i kalo (taro patch) as part of a summer program at Waimea. Photo 1984.*

The variety of classes, projects and services offered the community was impressive. Canoe building workshops, reading tutorial services, alternative education projects for alienated teenagers and summer enrichment classes were well-attended by the Hawaiian community. Part-Hawaiian graduates of the state's public schools took advantage of $500,000 in scholarships offered by Kamehameha's Nā Hoʻokama A Pauahi program.

In addition, Kamehameha conducted environmental projects such as the replanting of koa forests on the island of Hawaiʻi. Resource libraries of Hawaiian music and place names were developed, and the research and educational activities of other organizations such as Polynesian Voyaging Society and ʻAhahui ʻŌlelo Hawaiʻi were supported.

In twenty-three years of operation, 600,000 individuals had their lives enriched through Kamehameha's programs. By 1986, nearly 44,000 people on all major islands were served each year.

As the Kamehameha legacy was extended to the community, activities on the Kapālama campus remained diverse, enriching and vibrant.

Left: *Hawaiian history and culture are taught in a variety of ways, including poi pounding, in several summer programs. Photo 1980.*

Left: *Students display their best hula form in a 1981 summer program for high achievers.*

Left: *Rappelling is taught to encourage students to accept challenges in a boarding leadership course offered during the summer. Photo 1985.*

Right: *Students at Kalakaua Intermediate School in the Nā Pua A Pauahi reading tutorial program learn how to make sennit, twine made from tough coconut husk fibers, from Kamehameha reading teacher Ruby Lowe in 1985.*

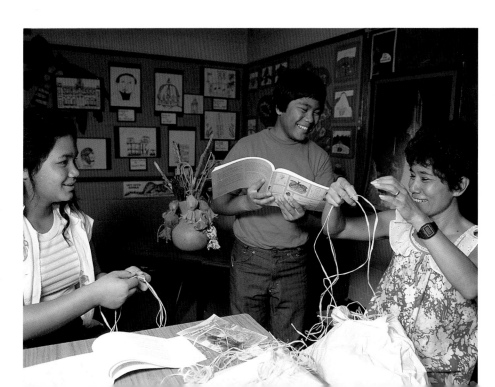

Another major focus of off-campus programs was on developing language arts skills. In 1971, the Kamehameha Early Education Project (KEEP) was established to develop improved ways to teach elementary-aged Hawaiian children reading and writing. KEEP pioneered curriculum and teaching techniques that are compatible with the cultural needs of Hawaiian children.

Efforts to strengthen the Schools' early education base included the changeover of Kamehameha's elementary division to a demonstration site in 1979. Students were admitted by random selection rather than ability. "I've been fortunate to be at Kamehameha during these exciting years," says Kahele Kukea, Class of 1963, elementary school principal. "It was a wonderful opportunity for me to work with administrators like Marian Welz and Sherlyn Franklin. I think we have succeeded in helping Hawaiian children to understand what they read."

As significant progress was made, the early education efforts continued to grow in size and scope. KEEP staff included anthropologists, sociologists, psychologists, and others who were able to view the child from many different aspects. Their research led Kamehameha to work with pre-kindergarten children and their families.

By 1983, KEEP was one of three early education programs under the Center for Development of Early Education (CDEE). The other two programs provide prenatal and preschool services to Hawaiian families, and program development services.

Above: *The observation deck at the demonstration school on campus allows educational researchers, student teachers and visiting educators to observe the effectiveness of teaching techniques. Photo circa 1982.*

Right: *Beautiful weather makes it possible to move outdoors for lessons. Photo 1983.*

KS-EARLY EDUCATION COMPLEX
THE KAMEHAMEHA SCHOOLS/
BERNICE PAUAHI BISHOP ESTATE

ARCHITECT: WILSON OKAMOTO & ASSOCIATES, INC.
STRUCTURAL ENGINEER: WILSON OKAMOTO & ASSOCIATES, INC.
CIVIL ENGINEER: WILSON OKAMOTO & ASSOCIATES, INC.
SOILS ENGINEER: WALTER LUM ASSOCIATES, INC.
MECHANICAL ENGINEER: KENNETH THOM ASSOCIATES, LTD.
ELECTRICAL ENGINEER: NAKAMURA, OYAMA & ASSOCIATES, LTD.
ACOUSTICAL ENGINEER: Y. EBISU & ASSOCIATES, INC.
LANDSCAPE ARCHITECT: TONGG, CLARKE & MECHLER, INC.
GENERAL CONTRACTOR: NORDIC CONSTRUCTION, LTD.

*Elementary students decorate
construction barriers surrounding
the new early education complex.
Photo 1986.*

Above: *A National Aeronautics and Space Administration (NASA) representative explains the function of a space suit modeled by elementary student Amber Murray during a visit to the Schools in 1985.*

Right: *Youngsters are exposed to the latest technological advancements at an early age.*

" *I can see the difference. He and his brother are always arguing [about] who's going to read. So, I'm glad. At least they take an interest, not like our time. Before, I was trying to run away from reading, doing lessons. But as time goes, times change, yeah? Education is more important.* "

Parent of student enrolled in
KEEP, Pahoa Elementary, 1982

Below: *Elementary students share a happy moment. Photo 1983.*

Above: *Students at Ulupono, the preschool on the Kapālama campus, cooperate on a building project during play period. Photo 1985.*

Right: *An Ulupono teacher assists a child with her beginning science studies. Photo 1985.*

Left: *Kamehameha also operates preschools in Anahola, Kaua'i; Waihe'e, Maui; and Nānāika-pono and Nānākuli, O'ahu. Photo 1985.*

Below: *The Kupulani parent-infant program provides educational and health related services to children and their families from birth to age five. Photo 1985.*

The dancers moved in the strong, dramatic rhythms of *hula kahiko*. The *pahu* and the deep, melodious voice of the chanter spoke across the centuries as young, proud Hawaiians living in a modern age rediscovered their unique heritage. The audience of Kamehameha Schools students, faculty and guests at the He Ho'olaule'a assembly in 1974 were stunned. A select group of young men, clad only in the traditional Hawaiian *malo*, performed the ancient *hula* as never before in recent history. When the *pahu* beat signaled the end of the inspiring dance, the crowd burst into uproarious applause and strident cries of "*hana hou!*"

A deepening sense of ethnic pride touched Kamehameha Schools students in the seventies and eighties. They displayed a revived interest in learning their native language, the ancient *mele*, chants, arts and crafts and values.

Their role models were the ever increasing numbers of Kamehameha graduates and other young Hawaiians who joined the ranks of the Kamehameha faculty. In 1981, for the first time in the Schools' history, two graduates were serving as principals: Anthony Ramos for the secondary school; and Kahele Kukea for the elementary school.

Above: *The resurgence of interest in the Hawaiian sport of canoe racing has led to Kamehameha participating in ILH paddling events and involvement in koa canoe building statewide. Photo circa 1980.*

Right: *The Concert Glee Club has been invited to perform for many dignitaries visiting Hawai'i including heads of state such as Queen Elizabeth of England and Emperor Hirohito of Japan. Photo 1970.*

Other aspects of campus life were well-integrated with the renewed emphasis on Hawaiian culture—from membership on the deputation team to participation in any one of several sports, Kamehameha students had a wide choice of special interest activities to choose from. Speech clubs, inter-class debates and literary societies strengthened student writing and speaking skills while providing healthy competition. *Ka Naʻi Aupuni*, the school yearbook, and *Ka Mōʻī*, the school newspaper, provided creative literary opportunities for future writers and journalists. As Carleen Paresa, Class of 1985, remembers, "There were just so many things to do and be involved in at Kamehameha."

Above: *Annually, the high school drama club produces a children's play and offers a series of performances for the general public. Photo circa 1980.*

Below: *Kamehameha's band has earned national and international recognition. In 1987, it was invited to appear at the Royal Tournament in London, England.*

Involvement in Kamehameha's special events was another important source of ethnic pride for the students. The Founder's Day practice of visiting Mauna 'Ala, the Royal Mausoleum in Nu'uanu, stirred feelings of reverence and respect for Hawai'i's royal past. Traditional protocol was carefully observed on these occasions, and Paula Akana, Class of 1980, remembers that "Founder's Day created an exciting feeling...as though you were actually standing in the presence of Hawaiian *ali'i.*"

The musical skills of Kamehameha students earned them national and international honors. The Warrior band was rated among America's top ten bands by the National Bandmasters Association in 1980, and four years later, the Glee Club successfully competed at the Llangollen International Music Festival in Wales.

No single event became more identified with the awakening spirit of Hawaiian pride than Kamehameha's Song Contest, first established in 1920. The live television broadcasts of the annual contest, begun in 1968, vividly captured the talent, hard work and joy of being a Kamehameha Warrior.

Todd Apo, Class of 1985, can still remember "the importance and overwhelming pride" he felt the night his class won the Song Contest. The sense of accomplishment went well beyond class competition. "My best memories are of the time after the contest...when people who just minutes before were competing for awards, are congratulating each other on their performances. The spirit of unity that Song Contest created is something I will never forget."

Above: *Delmann Naipo leads his class at Song Contest in 1984.*

Left: *The Concert Glee Club performed for the Perry Como Christmas Show filmed in Hāna, Maui, 1985.*

Above: *In October 1986, Kamehameha Schools and Bishop Museum held a combined celebration and fundraiser, Hui ʻAna, on the museum grounds.*

A decade of Kamehameha students and their families will remember the spirit and enthusiasm that was generated each year by Hoʻolauleʻa. The Association of Teachers and Parents sponsored its first annual fundraiser for Kamehameha families, friends and the general public in 1978. The day-long event featured Hawaiian food, crafts, games, lectures and entertainment. The 15,000 people that filled the upper campus field that first year contributed some $28,000 for student enrichment activities.

Through these types of public celebrations and events, the image of the Schools was transformed in the community. Hawaiians increasingly viewed Kamehameha as a source of effective educational and cultural inspiration. A statewide survey conducted in 1978 concluded that "there was strong support and positive feelings about the work of the Schools."

Above: *Hui ʻAna offered a great variety of plants, food, educational and recreational activities for the thousands of people who attended over the two-day period.*

Below: Ethnic delicacies and specialties from the neighbor islands were offered in abundance.

Above: A boy tries to out-grimace a fearsome image of Kūkāʻilimoku, the Hawaiian god of war.

Below: Entertainers ranged from these pint-sized hula dancers to seasoned musical performers.

Kamehameha moved into the eighties with optimism and hope. Gains made during the seventies laid the foundation for an ambitious undertaking in the next decade: to raise the educational performance profile of Hawaiian children to a level equal to or better than children throughout the nation.

Commitments were made to assist Hawaiians throughout Hawai'i, and a report to the Trustees indicated that "to the degree that this is accomplished, all citizens in the state will benefit as well."

Mid-way through the decade, Kamehameha looked forward to celebrating its 100th anniversary in 1987. A Centennial committee was established to plan for the historic event, and commemorative events were well underway by the time school opened in September, 1986.

This once-in-a-lifetime occurrence in Kamehameha's history provided Kamehameha students, staff, parents and alumni the chance to reflect on past accomplishments with pride, and anticipate the future with confidence. It was a time to celebrate the living legacy of a beloved Hawaiian princess.

Below: *A special convocation service was held at Kawaiaha'o Church in November 1986. School staff, students, and representatives of congress and Hawaiian organizations attended to mark the beginning of Kamehameha's Centennial school year.*

Above: To commemorate the Centennial, three coins were designed and minted for the Schools. Governor John Waihee and Lt. Governor Ben Cayetano joined Trustee Richard Lyman at the minting of the first coin honoring Kamehameha I in December 1986.

Above: The Pauahi coin was the second in the set of three commemorative coins to be minted in bronze, silver and gold. The third coin, honoring Charles Reed Bishop, will be issued in January of 1988.

Left: In remembrance of the tamarind tree planted at Pauahi's birth, a tamarind was placed in the courtyard of the new Bernice Pauahi Bishop Memorial Chapel. Photo 1986.

Above: *Members of the Class of 1979 rejoice in their Song Contest victory.*

"*Ultimately, the most enduring and enriching form of wealth is that of the spirit. Pauahi's legacy is the* mana *of her goodness — mana forever limitless, renewable, and accessible to all.*"

George Kanahele,
Class of 1948,
from *Pauahi, the Kamehameha Legacy,* 1986.

Above: *For Keala Pasco, and other members of the class of 1987, graduation is an ending and a new beginning.*

After a century, Kamehameha Schools bore little resemblance to that first hot, arid Pālama campus where a handful of teachers taught their Hawaiian students the skills and moral principals needed to survive in 20th century Hawai'i. Kamehameha had evolved into an educational institution with the facilities and resources to enrich the lives of thousands of Hawaiians throughout the islands.

Yet there remained a common bond between the past and present—the vision of Princess Pauahi to provide the children of Hawai'i with educational opportunities that would lead to fulfilling, productive lives. As Kamehameha Schools prepared for the next one hundred years, it sought strength and inspiration from her vision and expressed gratitude for her enduring gift.

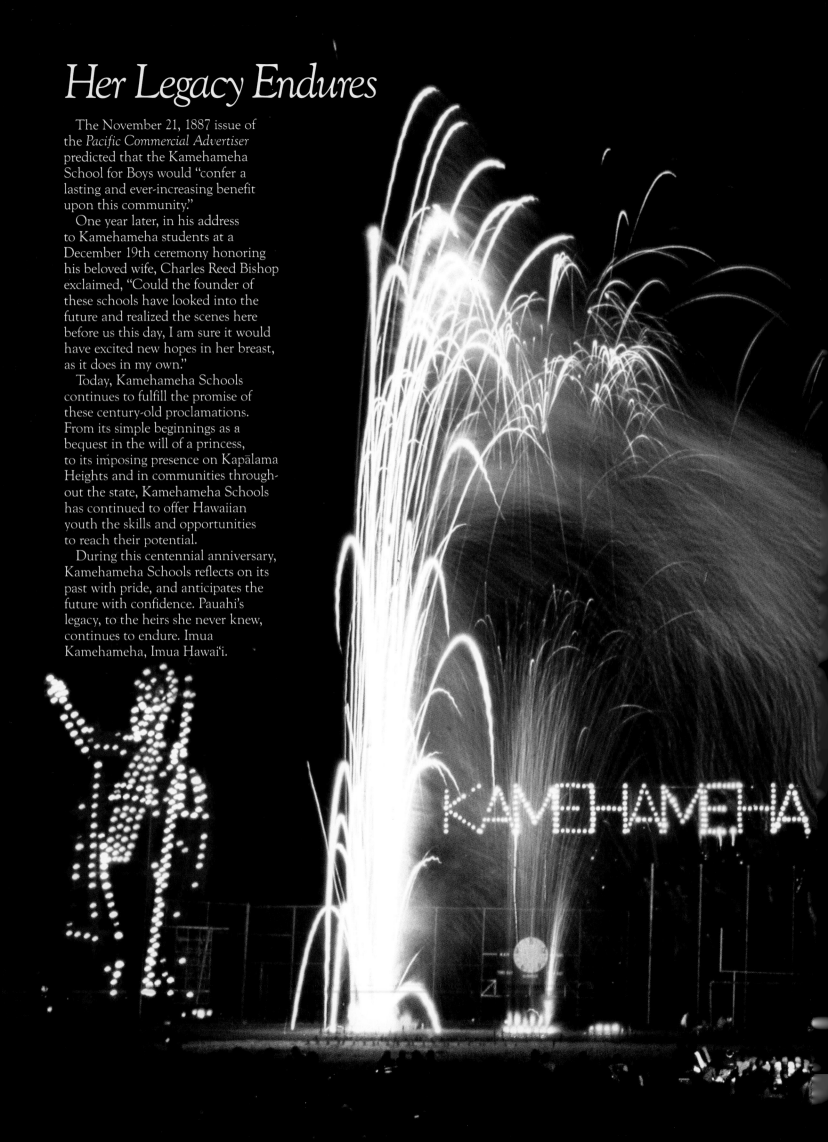

Her Legacy Endures

The November 21, 1887 issue of the *Pacific Commercial Advertiser* predicted that the Kamehameha School for Boys would "confer a lasting and ever-increasing benefit upon this community."

One year later, in his address to Kamehameha students at a December 19th ceremony honoring his beloved wife, Charles Reed Bishop exclaimed, "Could the founder of these schools have looked into the future and realized the scenes here before us this day, I am sure it would have excited new hopes in her breast, as it does in my own."

Today, Kamehameha Schools continues to fulfill the promise of these century-old proclamations. From its simple beginnings as a bequest in the will of a princess, to its imposing presence on Kapālama Heights and in communities throughout the state, Kamehameha Schools has continued to offer Hawaiian youth the skills and opportunities to reach their potential.

During this centennial anniversary, Kamehameha Schools reflects on its past with pride, and anticipates the future with confidence. Pauahi's legacy, to the heirs she never knew, continues to endure. Imua Kamehameha, Imua Hawai'i.

CELEBRATES
100 YEARS

HISTORICAL LISTING OF ADMINISTRATORS

Kamehameha School for Boys

William B. Oleson	1887–1893
Theodore Richards	1893–1898
Uldrick Thompson	1898–1901
Charles B. Dyke	1901–1904
Perley L. Horne	1904–1914
Ernest C. Webster	1914–1915
Charles R. Bostwick	1915–1918
Frank M. Watson	1918–1919
Earle G. Bartlett	1919–1922
Willard E. Givens	1922–1923
J. E. Carpenter	1923–1923
John M. Midkiff	1923–1924
John H. Nelson	1924–1930
Homer F. Barnes	1930–1944
Charles T. Parrent	1944–1946
Leonard Calvert	1946–1949
Allen A. Bailey	1949–1953
Oscar F. Fowler	1953–1954
Allen A. Bailey *(2nd appointment)*	1954–1966
R. Burl Yarberry	1966–1968
John E. Helfrich	1968–1969
Murl W. Anderson	1969–1970

Kamehameha School for Girls

Ida M. Pope	1894–1914
Frances A. Lemmon	1914–1915
Abbie H. Newton	1915–1927
Maude E. Schaeffer	1927–1942
Pauline M. Frederick	1942–1959
Margaret L. Hotaling	1959–1963
Gladys A. Brandt	1963–1970

Kamehameha Secondary School

Murl W. Anderson	1970–1972
Winona E. Rubin *(Acting)*	1972–1972
James J. Harpstrite	1972–1976
Diana Nui *(Acting)*	1976–1977
Anthony Ramos	1977–

Kamehameha Preparatory Department

Carrie A. Reamer	1888–1889
Nancy J. Malone	1889–1894
Alice E. Knapp	1894–1909
Florence E. Perrot	1909–1910
Alice E. Knapp *(2nd appointment)*	1910–1920
Maude Post	1920–1932
Lela R. Brewer	1943–1960
Richard L. Cundy	1960–1965
Diana H. Lord *(grades 7-8 only)*	1965–1982

Kamehameha Elementary Division (K-6)

Marian Welz	1965–1982
Kahele Kukea	1982–1985

Ka Naʻi Pono School (K-3)

Sherlyn Franklin	1974–1979
Sarah Sueoka	1979–1986

Kamehameha Elementary School (K-6)

Sherlyn Franklin	1979–1981
Kahele Kukea	1981–

PHOTOGRAPHIC CREDITS

CHAPTER I
Good and Industrious Men and Women
Kamehameha Schools Archives: All pages
James Putt: Will *Bruce Lum:* Page 7 bottom right

Pauahi O Kalani
Kamehameha Schools Archives: Page 20–21 background, 23 bottom right
Luryier Diamond: Page 20 bottom, 21 top, 22 top and bottom right
Bruce Lum: Page 20 top, 21 center and bottom, 22–23 background, 23 top and center
James Putt: Page 22 center

CHAPTER II
Kamehameha on the Move
Kamehameha Schools Archives: All pages

Esprit de Corps
Kamehameha Schools Archives: Page 38–39 background, 38 top, 40 center
Luryier Diamond: Page 38 bottom left, 39 top, 40–41 background, 40 top and bottom,
41 bottom
Jeff De Ponte: Page 41 top
Bruce Lum: Page 38 bottom right

CHAPTER III
Warriors in the Modern World
Kamehameha Schools Archives: Page 44, 45, 46, 47
Luryier Diamond: Page 42, 43, 48, 49, 50, 51, 52, 54, 55, 56, 57 top, 58, 59, 60, 61, 62, 63, 64, 65
bottom left, 67 bottom, 68 top and center, 69, 70, 71, 72, 73, 74
Bruce Lum: Page 57 bottom right, 65 top right
Student Photographers: Page 53, 57 bottom left (William Like KS '64), 65 bottom right, 66,
67 top, 68 bottom right

I mua Kamehameha
Kamehameha Schools Archives: Page 76 top, 78 top left and right
Luryier Diamond: Page 77 bottom, 77–78 background, 78 bottom, 79 bottom
Jeff De Ponte: Page 76 bottom, 77 top
Bruce Lum: Page 79 top
Student Photographer: Page 76–77 background (Charles Apo KS '57)

CHAPTER IV
Challenges at the Campus Gate
Luryier Diamond: Page 81, 84, 85, 86, 87, 88, 89, 90, 91, 92, 93, 94, 95, 96 top, 97, 98,
99 top, 100, 101, 103, 104, 105, 106, 107
Student Photographers: Page 80, 82, 83 top and bottom left (all Cedric Ludington KS '61),
83 bottom right (Julian Ako KS '61), 96 bottom, 99 bottom (Abraham Maioho KS '64), 102
(Bruce Lum KS '65)

Kamehameha Sings
Kamehameha Schools Archives: Page 108 center
Luryier Diamond: Page 108–109 background, 109 top, 110–111 background, 110 bottom,
111 top left
Bruce Lum: Page 108 top and bottom, 109 bottom, 110 top left and right, 111 top right
and bottom

CHAPTER V
The Vision Burns Bright
Luryier Diamond: Page 134 bottom
Bruce Lum: Page 112, 114 top left and right, 115 top, 116 bottom, 119 top and bottom, 121 top, 123
top, 124, 125, 126, 127 bottom, 128 bottom, 129, 130, 131, 132, 133, 135 bottom, 136, 137, 138,
139, 140, 141, 143
Jeff De Ponte: Page 114 bottom, 115 bottom, 117 top and bottom right, 118, 119 center, 120, 122,
123 bottom, 127 top and center, 134 top, 135 top, 142
Dave Au: Page 121 bottom
James Putt: Page 117 bottom right
Larry Loganbill: Page 128 top

Studio: Page 113 inset (Sterling's Fotografiks), 116 top (Damien Waring negative donated to
Kamehameha by Mrs. Marjorie Midkiff)
Design Elements: Page 114 top left (haku lei fashioned by Lana Costa), 55 and 65 (athletic,
academic honors and citizenship pins loaned by Julia Stewart Williams KS '46), 121 (hula
implements loaned by Puanani Fernandez-Akamine KS '78), 143 (ring loaned by Robert Lindsey
KS '65)

Her Legacy Endures
James Putt: Page 144–145
Bruce Lum: Dustjacket flap top photo
James Putt: Dustjacket flap bottom photo